MARCO  POLO

Tips

CAPE VERDE

Azores (P)

Madeira (P)

Canary Islands (E)   MOROCCO

ATLANTIC
OCEAN   Western
                     Sahara

Cape Verde   MAURITANIA

                SENEGAL

www.marco-polo.com

SYMBOLS

INSIDER TIP Insider Tip
★ Highlight
●●●● Best of ...
🌿 Scenic view
☺ Responsible travel: fair trade principles and the environment respected

PRICE CATEGORIES HOTELS

Expensive over 8800 CVE
Moderate 4400–8800 CVE
Budget under 4400 CVE

The prices are for a night in a double room with breakfast

PRICE CATEGORIES RESTAURANTS

Expensive over 1300 CVE
Moderate 800–1300 CVE
Budget under 800 CVE

The prices are for a main course without drinks

On the cover: Banana leaf lamps p. 90 | Up to the Pico do Fogo p. 102

CONTENTS

Northern islands → p. 76

Trips & Tours → p. 100

Sports & Activities → p. 106

Road atlas → p. 128

DID YOU KNOW?

MAPS IN THE GUIDEBOOK

(130 A1) Page numbers and coordinates refer to the road atlas
(0) Site/address located off the map
Coordinates are also given for places that are not marked on the road atlas
Street maps of Praia and Mindelo can be found inside the back cover

INSIDE BACK COVER: PULL-OUT MAP →

PULL-OUT MAP 🗺

(🗺 A–B 2–3) Refers to the removable pull-out map

The best MARCO POLO Insider Tips

Our top 15 Insider Tips

INSIDER TIP **Magical spot above the waves**
Dinner in the O Farolim Restaurant in Santa Maria with the sound of the sea in the background is an unforgettable experience → p. 37

INSIDER TIP **Coffee in style**
In the elegant Canta Morna café on Boavista you can enjoy the best Italian coffee and delicious homemade cakes → p. 45

INSIDER TIP **Sundowner with the surge of the surf**
A beach of white sand, the crash of the surf and the sun sinks majestically into the sea ... the Tortuga Beach Club on Boavista satisfies all your sunset fantasies → p. 46

INSIDER TIP **Undiscovered beach with silvery sands**
The palm fringed Praia da Prata on Santiago with its dark, fine sand is a little known gem off the beaten tourist track → p. 62

INSIDER TIP **The way the wind blows**
Discover the islands onboard the two-master 'Iceni Queen', visit isolated beaches and dive into the cool ocean from the deck of the boat → p. 108

INSIDER TIP **Veils of mist in the fairytale forest**
The diffused sunlight and ethereal veils of mist conjure up a mystical world in the Monte Velha nature reserve on Fogo → p. 65

INSIDER TIP **Wonderful culinary delights**
Excellent cuisine, friendly and attentive service in a relaxed atmosphere – be pampered in the Santo André Restaurant in São Pedro → p. 82

INSIDER TIP **Fresh from the barrel**
Down-to-earth fun: the tiny tavern in the market hall of the *mercado municipal* in Mindelo (photo above) is definitely not a tourist trap – and it's the perfect place to enjoy a fresh draught beer! → p. 82

INSIDER TIP Vivid parrots on a tropical patio

The Orquidea Guesthouse on Boavista is a green paradise where the guests, dogs and parrots are all treated as part of the family. Breakfast is served in their beautiful tropical courtyard → p. 47

INSIDER TIP Tranquil sea, peace and quiet

The charming Mar Tranquilidade Guesthouse with its simple, thatched stone cottages on Santo Antão is a secluded oasis of calm – and the food served here is also quite outstanding → p. 93

INSIDER TIP Culinary delights and a special attraction

Cape Verde culture meets Senegalese culinary art – experience both in Pipi's Bar on Fogo. The owner serves spicy, fragrant West African dishes and there is live music on Friday evenings → p. 68

INSIDER TIP French Creole cooking with a view

A French chef serves wonderful food to match the spectacular scenery in the courtyard of the Pousada Pedra Brabo in the Cha das Caldeiras → p. 103

INSIDER TIP Absolutely pure!

In the verdantly tropical Paúl Valley Cape Verde's purest *grogue* is produced according to Tyrolean distillery standards → p. 105

INSIDER TIP Turtle adventure

Get up close and personal with theses rare animals – with the SOS Tartarugas rangers (photo below) → p. 110

INSIDER TIP Kingfishers outside the bedroom window

Kingfishers dive and butterflies flutter past the windows of your room in the Quinta da Montanha Pousada Quinta da Montanha mountain lodge – and the views are stunning → p. 64

BEST OF ...

GREAT PLACES FOR FREE
Discover new places and save money

● *Full moon festival*
Entrance to the *music festival in Baía das Gatas* is free! Every year bands from Cape Verde, Africa and Latin America perform for three days – on the first weekend in August after full moon – on São Vicente's most famous beach → p. 113

● *Into the water!*
If you decide to have Sunday lunch in the four star *Resort Hotel Foya Branca* on São Vicente, you will dine in style and then be able to relax in and around the hotel's pools free of charge ... → p. 111

● *Aide-memoire*
Monique Widmer has been collecting historical objects and documents dealing with everyday life on the Cape Verdes – especially on Fogo – for more than 25 years. Furniture, household effects, old photos and other exhibits tell the turbulent history of the islands in her *Casa da Memória*, and there is no admission charge → p. 67

● *Birthday celebration*
Live music galore – Cape Verde's capital city Praia celebrates the anniversary of its foundation on 19 May. To mark the occasion, dozens of bands and thousands of visitors come together to celebrate for three days at the free concerts given on the *Praia de Gamboa* → p. 113

● *A little night music*
Live music as a free extra with your dinner – this is the *noite caboverdeana* in Mindelo – where you can dine, chat and enjoy the soulful background music as an accompaniment → p. 84

● *Sunday rhythm*
A brass band sets the tone on the *Praça Nova* (photo) every Sunday afternoon in Mindelo. It is a tradition to put on your Sunday best and go for a leisurely stroll to see and be seen → p. 80

●●●● Dots in guidebook refer to 'Best of ...' tips

● *Travel with the locals*

The *aluguer* is the most common means of transportation on Cape Verde. You should travel at least once with the locals in one of these pickups, such as the trip from *São Filipe* to *Chã das Caldeiras* → p. 102

● *Swing those hips*

You won't know what has hit you when the dancers start swinging their hips at a dizzy speed dancing the *batuco* in the *Sal da Música* in Praia → p. 62

● *A hearty pleasure*

The Cape Verde national dish *catchupa* is a hearty affair. Every cook prepares their own different version of this stew made of sweet corn and beans – in the *Churrasqueira Africana* on Fogo they add pumpkin → p. 68

● *New braids*

Men, women and children wear their hair woven into small braids. If you want to do the same, you can have your holiday hairstyle done in the *shop next to the Mariama Restaurant* in Vila do Maio → p. 51

● *Pure firewater*

No matter whether it is freshly distilled or aged, the Cape Verde sugar cane liquor packs a punch! The freshly brewed firewater *(grogue novo)* that is served in the *Pavilhão* on the Praça Nova in Mindelo and elsewhere will really take your breath away! → p. 85

● *Strategic moves*

A typical scene: two men sitting in the shade with a wooden board between them pondering over how they can get as many small pieces as possible away from their opponent. The game is called *oril* and it attracts many players to the *row of shops near the sport stadium* in Sal Rei and numerous other places on the islands → p. 45

● *Glittering catch*

At midday everybody runs to see if the fishermen have made a good catch when their colourful boats return to port or are pulled up on to the beach – as they do in *Tarrafal* on Santiago (photo) → p. 64

ONLY IN

BEST OF ...

● *Bygone era*
You will get a good idea of Fogo's everyday life of yesteryear in the cool rooms of the *Museu Municipal de São Filipe*. The film of the volcano eruption in 1995 is well worth seeing; it is unfortunately only in Portuguese and the sound is not the best, but it is the pictures that count ... → p. 67

● *From fishing lines to dentures*
Sucupira is a type of local market for clothes, shoes, electronic equipment, CDs, household utensils, car supplies and much more. There is plenty to see and you can often find lovely things. The largest covered *sucupira* is in *Praia* → p. 59

● *Peace, quiet and culture*
The airy courtyard in the *Centro Cultural* in Mindelo is the perfect place to sit down and relax or take a closer look at one of the changing exhibitions. A small shop sells a wide selection of Cape Verde handicrafts → p. 82

● *Music in the air*
Listen to the melodies of the many popular Cape Verdean musicians, compare the artists and their styles and then select the music that suits your taste in one of the air-conditioned shops. There is a fine selection in the specialist *Harmonia* shops on Santiago and elsewhere → p. 61

● *Devotion and fervour*
When did you last go to church? Take part in mass at *Nossa Senhora da Graça* (photo) in Praia and you will be amazed at how the faithful follow the sermon so intently → p. 58

● *Trees and flowers*
A stroll through the *Botanical Gardens* in São Jorge dos Orgãos offers you the chance to become familiar with endemic plants, medicinal herbs and various tree species → p. 59

HEAT

RELAX AND CHILL OUT
Take it easy and spoil yourself

● *Don't disturb the peace*
No telephone, no internet and television and mobile phones are also taboo. The beach, silence and solitude are the motto of the *Spinguera Ecolodge* on Boavista – miles from anywhere → **p. 48**

● *Go with the flow!*
You can't sink if you swim in the salt pans of the *salt works* (photo) at Pedra de Lume on Sal – just float! Your skin will also welcome the salty bath → **p. 35**

● *Colonial lifestyle*
Sink into the gigantic wicker chairs, take a sip of your fruity cocktail and listen to the water splashing in the fountain. In the background, the dulcet tones of Cape Verdean music ... The *Fogo Lounge* in São Filipe is the place to chill out in style → **p. 69**

● *Born again*
It is like a fountain of youth: a traditional Balinese massage with the finest aromatic body oils guarantees that you will soon feel like a new person. The treatments offered by the therapist Prem Piepiet in the *Oásis Atlântico Porto Grande Hotel* regenerate both body and soul → **p. 86**

● *Deckchair at the marina*
The *Bar Pont' Água* in the bustling centre of Mindelo is the perfect place to take a break. Either with a short stop to catch your breath over a cool drink at the bar or a longer one with a deckchair and quick dip in the swimming pool. No matter which you choose, there is always the lovely view of the marina to admire → **p. 85**

● *Sundowner with the play of the waves*
As the sun sinks like a gigantic red ball into the ocean enjoy the wonderful light and warmth, have a chat or just let your thoughts wander ... The *Panorama* hotel bar on Santiago is an ideal place to let your day draw to a close → **p. 60**

INTRODUCTION

DISCOVER CAPE VERDE!

Cape Verde is all about colour: the turquoise ocean, lush tropical valleys, beaches of black and white sand, the bright yellow of the bananas, the orange-coloured papayas, green heads of cabbage and red peppers. And then there are the people who live here: there are all shades of skin colour imaginable from lily white to coffee to dark brown with sparkling eyes in all shades of green, blue and brown – a fascinating mixture! Cape Verdeans also love brightly coloured clothes – with as much glitter as possible – and you shouldn't be surprised to see young men wearing sparkling neck-laces and earrings. However, it is not only the popular costume jewellery that is dazzling – there are many different facets to life on the Cape Verde Islands.

Colourful fishing boats lie on the white sandy beaches, the deep blue ocean glitters as far as the eye can see, a gentle breeze cools off the scorching sun. The village square and the narrow cobbled streets seem to be deserted; only a few children can be seen playing with toys they have made themselves. However, there is a lot of hustle and

Photo: São Pedro Bay on São Vicente

Sand dunes on Boavista, the 'Sahara of Cape Verde'

bustle at the vegetable market – the centre and heart of every village – loud shouting and laughter, friendly faces and mountains of fresh fruit. Women squat on the roadside with baskets full of silvery fish, a group of men sit in the shade of a tree playing cards. Life here is leisurely and relaxed, people have time and they also have patience.

> **The quiet serenity of the people is remarkable**

The quiet serenity of the Cape Verdean people is remarkable and this is despite the fact that life here is so hard that two thirds of the population live abroad.

The name Cabo Verde – the green cape – is misleading as the archipelago in the Atlantic Ocean (460km/285mi off the west coast of Africa) is anything but green. The

155mi² group of 15 islands lies on the fringe of the Sahel zone and suffers from extreme heat and aridity.

There is only sufficient water for agriculture on five of the nine inhabited islands – and that is only if the annual rainfall actually materializes. Ninety per cent of the food has to be imported – and this figure is growing. The four other islands are bone dry; brown deserts where the few solitary mountains are not able to halt the clouds brought by the constant north-easterly wind. The islands are categorised as being windward *(barlavento)* or leeward *(sotavento)* or by their geographic location:

> Each island group – and each individual island – is different

three flat, desert-like, eastern islands and the three mountainous north and south islands. Each island group, and each island, is different. The eastern islands of Sal, Boavista and Maio have magnificent white sandy beaches and are a paradise for water sports enthusiasts. In the north are Santo Antão and São Nicolau with spectacular mountain panoramas and tropical valleys, while São Vicente is famous for Mindelo its bustling port metropolis. The main islands in the south are Santiago, with the capital city, the almost 3000m/9840ft high volcanic island Fogo and the secluded, peaceful Brava.

The first settlement on the formerly uninhabited islands was established in 1461 by seafarers sailing under the flag of the Portuguese king. Within a few decades as a Portuguese overseas colony, Cape Verde developed into the hub of the slave trade

1810 First salt works on Boavista

1838 Start of the salt trade on Sal

1885 Mindelo is a relay station for the first transatlantic telegraph cable

1956 Founding of the PAIGC (African Party for the Independence of Guinea-Bissau and Cape Verde)

1975 Political independence granted to the Portuguese colony. The PAIGC is the only party and governs the young nation

between Africa, Europe and America. White settlers from Europe came into contact with an increasing stream of slaves from Africa and their children formed the first generation of a new people: the Creoles. The genes, customs and traditions of two continents produced a population with just as many skin colours as characteristic culture and lifestyle. The Creole culture is colourful and full of vitality – in its emotional music, its dances and everyday customs. The Creoles then made their way from Cape Verde to South America and into the Caribbean. You will not only experience the exuberant joie de vivre of the carnival parades with beautiful dancers in magnificent feather costumes there – just travel to Mindelo on São Nicolau!

It is not really contradictory that a great number of Christian traditions have also found a place in Cape Verdean life. The Cape Verdeans are extremely fond of spectacular masses and processions and celebrate a great number of religious festivals with cheerful enthusiasm and real enjoyment.

More Cape Verdeans live abroad than on the islands themselves

Almost half of the islands' population of 470,000 live on Santiago, of which 130,000 are in the capital city of Praia. Around 800,000 Cape Verdeans live abroad; mainly in the United States, Portugal, France and West Africa. Many people perished from the repeated droughts and famines in the 1940s and many more were forced to emigrate or sell themselves into slavery so as not to starve. That is why the generation of 55 to 70 year olds is almost entirely absent today. The current average age is just 20 years.

Until a few years ago, the Cape Verde Islands were one of the poorest countries on earth. After 500 years of Portuguese exploitation, the country gained political independence in 1975. The independence pioneer was the Cape Verdean freedom fighter Amílcar Cabral, who was involved in the founding of the PAIGC independence party in 1956. He was assassinated in 1973 but has remained an important figure in the political and social life of Cape Verde. It was only after the end of the colonial era that the country, which had been extremely neglected under the fascist dictatorship of Salazar (1928–74), was able to gradually recover from its systematic exploitation. There has been a democratic, multiparty system in place since 1991 and Cape Verde is a pluralist-parliamentary republic.

1981
Political separation from Guinea-Bissau; PAIGC renamed PAICV

1990
Multiparty system introduced

1991
First democratic parliamentary elections; victory of the MPD (Movement for Democracy)

2001
The PAICV takes over government once again; Pedro Pires named President

2011
The PAICV wins the parliamentary elections but Jorge Carlos Fonseca (MPD) becomes new President

Attractive remnants of the colonial era: church and houses in Mindelo

A political and economic change has taken place in the last 30 years, one that has made it possible for the country to overcome hunger and poverty. Tourism plays an extremely important role with the islands of Sal and Boavista currently being equipped with the infrastructure necessary to attract even more tourists than before to the Cape Verde Islands. The mountainous islands of the archipelago are becoming increasingly attractive for tourists with more facilities being set up for holidaymakers.

In addition to the characteristic features of the individual island groups there is also the colonial architecture – that dates back to the 17th–19th centuries – that is another attraction for visitors. The build-

The buildings decorated in bright pastel colours

ings are in a wide range of pastel tones and make history just as colourful as Cape Verde's culture and traditions. Maintaining their traditions, especially their music, is considered vital to Cape Verdeans. This makes it possible for them to not only survive in an inhospitable environment but to live their lives in admirable dignity and happiness. Make sure that you have enough time, and curiosity, to be able to get involved with these people and their colourful world.

WHAT'S HOT

1 Without canvas

Art Was it born of necessity or is it proof of creativity? The island artists do not limit themselves to a single medium. Video, photographs and the traditional canvas are the materials *Djon Brito (djonbrito.tripod.com)* makes use of in his work. The works of the painter and video artist Fernando Hamilton Barbosa Elias alias *Mito (www.tanboru.org/mito, photo)* can be found in some surprising places such as on a house wall. More island art can be viewed at *Zero Point Art (Mindelo, Rua Unidade Africana 62)*.

Musical 2

Sodade Longing, known as *sodade*, is the defining theme of the island music called *morna*. Suzanna Lubrano *(www.suzannalubrano.com, photo)* is a master of the genre; she gave up her Cape Verdean homeland and found homesickness. The musician Maria de Barros *(mariadebarros.com)* tries to make sure that as many children as possible have access to instruments in her *Salt (salt.nimekula.org)* project and in so doing preserves the country's musical tradition. Visitors can get a real taste of the local music in the *Bar Clube Nautica* at the harbour in Mindelo.

3 Santiago spectacular

Architecture Nature is no longer the main draw card, César Freitas *(www.ffcb.pt, photo)* builds spectacular hotels on Santiago. Carlo Hamelberg, on the other hand, designs colourfully cheerful residential buildings such as the *Residência João Gomes (Praia, www.hamelberg.com)*. And Pedro Lopez's *(www.arq-pelo.de)* clear design for a commercial building in Praia complements the imposing landscape of Santiago.

Standing on water

Stand up paddling   Michael Forbes has played a major role in making stand up paddling, or SUP for short, so popular on the Cape Verde Islands. Ever since he paddled his way around the island of Sal for a good cause, many others have wanted to try their hand at the sport. *Ed Angulo (Santa Maria, www.angulocabo verde.com)* not only offers surfboards but now also the more stable SUP boards. Mitu Monteiros and Djo Silvas' *M&D Kite School (Santa Maria, www.kite schoolcaboverde.com)* has a similar offer. If there is no wind, many surfers switch to SUP and some of them get really hooked. Sal is not the only location with ideal conditions for this meditative, yet quite strenuous, sport. The bay off Sal Rei on Boavista is just one of the many other good spots.

Sleep well

Archetypal   An increasing number of typical island homes and architectural gems from the colonial era are now being spruced up and turned into exquisite hotels. These include the *Cabo Verde Palace (Santa Maria, Sal)* with its impressive façade and the comfortable *Villa Botanico (Tarrafal, Santiago, photo)*. Although its two rooms are not historical, you will still feel like you are living in a manor house and will be able to spend wonderfully relaxing days in the tropical garden or lounging around the swimming pool. In contrast, you will get a real feel for Cape Verdean life in the *House of Isabel (Cova Joana, Brava)*. The simple guesthouse in Brava, surrounded by fields and farmhouses, is the perfect starting point for hikes in the countryside!

IN A NUTSHELL

A LUGUER
The *aluguer* (Portuguese: to rent) is the most characteristic mode of transport in Cape Verde: private vehicles with several seats that travel between villages. Mini-buses are used for longer trips and open pickups with benches for shorter distances. The drivers pick up passengers at specific stops and also en route. If necessary, you will have to budge up to make room for new passengers – the vehicle is only full when there are 15 people on board ...

B EGGING
Many families live from hand to mouth and many children have neither exercise books nor pens. This knowledge means that some tourists slip a little something to begging children: a cheap ballpoint pen, a few sweets or maybe even a coin or two. However, that does more harm than good as it encourages dependence and the idea that begging is an easy and successful way to make a living. If you really want to help, make a donation of money or in kind to a recognised institution or a welfare project such as *www.delta cultura.org/en.*

B RAIDS
Regardless of sex or age many men, women and children have their hair woven

Photo: Carnival in Mindelo

Irrepressible joie de vivre and insatiable longing: varied cultures and passionate feelings – from *morabeza* to *sodade*

into small braids *(tranças)*. There are endless variations of hairstyles and if the locals get tired of their style after a few days, they simply have a new one done. The ends of the little braids are usually decorated with colourful plastic beads.

CLIMATE

The dry tropical climate makes Cape Verde an ideal year-round holiday desti-
nation. On average there are 350 days of sunshine a year, with temperatures between 21–29°C/70–84°F. January and February are the coolest months and it is particularly hot in August and September. During this period there are often heavy tropical downpours but the trade winds are less strong from July to October. There is only a slight difference between the day and night temperatures – around 5°C/9°F.

The peaks keep the rain clouds at bay on the mountainous islands

The water temperature ranges from 22–27°C/72–80°F.

DISCOTHEQUES

European-style discotheques are only in the areas where a lot of people live or where there are many tourists – in Praia, Mindelo and Santa Maria. In the villages and small towns, rooftop terraces are often transformed into discos at the weekend: hot rhythms and cool drinks turn any flat roof into a dance floor. Just follow the sound of the music ...

EMIGRATION

Famine and drought were the undesired companions that Cape Verdeans had to live with for 500 years and what forced many people to leave the islands. In the 19th century, the first young men signed on to the American whaling ships that stocked up on supplies at Cape Verde. Since then there have been close ties to the east coast of the United States and there are now around 500,000 people of Cape Verde descent living in the United States – the total worldwide is about 700,000. Cape Verde would not be able to survive without its emigrants. Sixty to seventy per cent of the families on the islands receive financial support from relatives living abroad. Even today, most of the young people still dream about America and Europe where they believe they will be able to make a lot of money. Many Cape Verdeans who have lived and worked abroad for years are now investing their money in their home country. Especially in the area of tourism where a number of small enterprises have been established and are now making a major contribution to the positive tourist development of Cape Verde.

FAMILY

Women are the backbone of Cape Verde society. Only 16 per cent of the people living on the islands are married, most are either in a long-standing relationship or describe themselves as being single (54 per cent). Family ties are very complicated as women often have several children from different men and many men have children with several women. They take on the role of father with their family of the moment and it is not usual to have several relationships at the same time. Many of the women have their first child while they are still very young and often have to bring their children up alone with – or without – financial support from the father.

G ROGUE

The Portuguese colonialists planted sugar cane and cotton and soon started trading in them. Until the beginning of the 18th century the entire sugar cane harvest was exported, then the farmers on Santo Antão started using it to distil rum (Creole: *grogue*). They used mobile sugar cane presses to extract the juice from the cane and then let it ferment in open barrels before distilling in large copper kilns. The freshly distilled clear liquor is known as *grogue novo* (new grog); after a minimum of three years of aging in a wooden barrel, this matures to *grogue velha* (old grog) which is light brown and far gentler and milder than the original firewater. *Grogue* has an alcohol content of around 40 per cent and is produced on all of the mountainous islands, but it is said that the best comes from Santo Antão.

K RIOLU

The national language Kriolu (Creole) is spoken in everyday life in Cape Verde while the official language is Portuguese. There are several variants of Kriolu, each island has its own dialect and there are major differences between the north and south islands, so the Kriolu spoken on Santiago differs strongly from the language on the northern islands. There is still no common form of writing; it is currently being developed. Kriolu was created out of several African languages and Portuguese, 90 per cent of the vocabulary is Portuguese but the grammar has African roots. In the 15th century Kriolu was an important lingua franca in the maritime field.

Early stage of *grogue*: sugar cane juice is extracted in large presses

MERCEARIA & BARBEARIA

The general store and the barber – there is one of each in every village. You will find an inconspicuous *mercearia*, a small grocery shop that sells just about everything and also acts as a bar, on almost every street corner. As one customer buys a bag of flour, a tablespoon of paprika or a couple of stock cubes, so another one lifts his glass of *grogue* to toast all those present. The *barbearia*, where men not only go for a haircut but also a shave, is often a little harder to find.

MORABEZA

The Cape Verdeans call their own special attitude towards life *morabeza*. It is impossible to provide a clear translation of the word but it encompasses a zest for life and joie de vivre, longing, love of one's homeland and a national feeling of belonging, dignity, hospitality, respect and kindness to others, the Creole culture and much more.

MUSIC

There is music everywhere – you will always hear a radio playing no matter whether you are in a taxi, a café, an office or at the beach. However, most of the music played is not originally Cape Verdean but *zouk* – modern electronic pop music introduced from the Caribbean islands of Martinique and Guadeloupe. The new Caribbean sounds were easily integrated into the local culture as previously happened with influences from West Africa, Portugal and Brazil.

The styles and instruments for traditional music differ from island to island and there are strong differences between the north and south islands. On the northern islands, you will usually hear melodic songs with poetic lyrics accompanied by a guitar, the four-sting *cavaquinho* or violin. The most important musical genres are the melancholic *morna* and the more cheerful *coladeira*. Thanks to Cesária Évora (who died in 2011) and her song 'Sodade', most Europeans have heard at least one *morna*. The singer made her first recording at the end of the 1980s at the age of 47 and became an international star within a few short years.

African elements dominate in the music in the south where the music is characterised by a kind of improvised question/answer form with a repetitious, drum-driven rhythmic structure. *Funaná, batuco* and *tabanka* are the most prominent forms. All of these styles of music have one thing in common; they invite participation rather than passive listening – all Cape Verdeans love singing, dancing and having fun.

NORTH-EAST TRADE WIND

The north-east trade wind blows strongly and steadily from October to July – a pleasantly cooling breeze that alleviates the omnipresent heat. Windsurfers on the flat eastern islands will feel like they are in paradise. The mountainous islands benefit even more: their peaks stop the clouds that the wind drives across the Atlantic and the moisture makes the north-eastern side of these islands green and fertile.

ORIL

Visitors will see the game of strategy *oril* (Creole: *urim*) being played on all of the islands. Two men, with an oblong wooden box with twelve hollows between them, sit in front of house doors, in cafés or in public squares. Each player has 24 balls (olive-green plant seeds) that he has to place in his and his opponents' hollows in a way that he can take them out again as quickly as possible. The winner is the first to have more than 24 balls in his possession.

RELIGION

Religion plays a very important role in Cape Verde life and about 80 per cent of the population are members of the Roman Catholic Church but other denominations are becoming increasingly popular. About 10 per cent are Protestants, about half of which are Nazarenes. The remainder are Jehovah's Witnesses, Mormons and Anglicans or belong to other religions.

SLAVE TRADE

Two factors set a chain of events in motion in the second half of the 15th century: Spain and Portugal discovered and colonised Africa and America, and a new foodstuff became fashionable in Europe – sugar. The gigantic sugar cane plantations in the newly acquired colonies were worked by slaves who were transported from the western coast of Africa in their thousands. Within just a few decades, a profitable three-way trade that cost millions of people their life came into being: weapons and manufactured goods to Africa, slaves to America and sugar and rum to Europe. Its strategic location made Cape Verde an important hub and Ribeira Grande rapidly developed into one of the most important trading centres of the slave trade. This nightmare lasted 350 years.

SODADE

The Cape Verdeans call the sense of irretrievable loss and unquenchable longing – for the distant homeland, a lost love, the family or the past – *sodade*. This bittersweet longing finds its main expression in melancholic *morna* songs.

TOURISM

The Cape Verde Islands are increasingly becoming the focus of interest of tourists. Consistently warm temperatures,

There is a Catholic church (seen here: Sal Rei) in almost every large town

magnificent beaches, exotic flair and their proximity to Europe make them a dream destination. The three eastern islands, with their white sand beaches and turquoise sea, are quite simply made for mass tourism and the construction industry and all-inclusive hotels are booming. The mountainous islands, with their steep coasts, are perfect for hiking and adventure holidays. Here, mainly small local enterprises benefit from the increase in the number of holidaymakers.

WATER

Nothing is more precious than water in Cape Verde. None of the islands has sufficient rainfall and the cisterns that can be seen everywhere have to be filled by tank trucks most of the time. In rural areas, water has to be collected from public outlets and taken home in plastic canisters on donkey back. Modern hotels have their own desalination plants to supply water. Do your bit and save as much water as you can!

FOOD & DRINK

The food served in Cape Verde depends entirely on the wherewithal. Poverty and wealth are mirrored on the dinner plate: maize and beans for some, lobsters for others.

The latter are naturally popular with gourmets and fortunately there are plenty of them in the seas off the islands. They are on offer in most restaurants – at affordable prices. The poor eat simple, yet nourishing meals. Cape Verdean cooks conjure up a variety of stews made of sweet corn, pulses and vegetables that are hardly any less varied than the wealth of seafood that comes from the Atlantic. Depending on the region certain ingredients are used, such

as pork and goat meat, for the regional specialities of the individual islands such as *modje* on São Nicolau and *djagacida* on Fogo.

Eating is always a social event: usually family, friends and neighbours all come together for a meal and a splendid feast is a must at any official or private celebration. *Cachupa* is the national dish of Cape Verde, a stew of sweet corn and beans that is refined with meat, sausage or fish – if available. *Cachupa* is served time and time again: first as a thick soup and then the next morning it is fried with onions and possibly an egg for breakfast. *Cachupa* is more than just a nourishing

Creole delicacies: all that the poor soil and rich fishing grounds can provide is served in countless variations

meal – it is part of the Cape Verdean life-style and creates an important aspect of the country's common identity.

Fish *(pexi)* is also frequently eaten. There are plenty of varieties in the ocean to enhance any meal: small fish such as *garoupa, cavala* and *bonito* are prepared whole, complete with head and bones; larger fish such as *serra, dorada, esmoregal* and tuna *(atum)* are served as fillets –

usually grilled. Seafood such as squid, mussels and other shellfish are always fresh and prepared in a variety of tasty ways. However, you should forgo the lobster during the closed season from July to November!

The fresh fish in Cape Verde is hard to beat and definitely preferable to meat *(kárni)* – especially if the chicken *(frángu)* comes from the deep freeze and not the cook's

LOCAL SPECIALITIES

▶ **Arroz de marisco** – rice with seafood
▶ **Arroz de peixe** – rice with one or more varieties of fish
▶ **Bife de atum** – tuna steak
▶ **Bife de serra** – swordfish steak (photo right)
▶ **Búzio** – whelks
▶ **Cabrito** – goat kid
▶ **Caldo de peixe** – fish soup
▶ **Canja de galinha** – chicken soup with rice
▶ **Cozido de peixe** – boiled fish with potatoes and vegetables
▶ **Doce de coco** – confection made with coconut and sugar
▶ **Doce de leite** – milk pudding
▶ **Doce de papaia** – fruit jelly made with preserved papaya
▶ **Feijoada** – hearty bean stew

▶ **Frango assado** – grilled chicken
▶ **Garopa** – perch (usually served whole), eat carefully as there are many fine bones!
▶ **Lagosta grelhada** – grilled lobster (photo left)
▶ **Lagosta soada** – lobster braised in a tomatoes and onion broth
▶ **Lapas** – mussels
▶ **Legumes cozido** – boiled vegetables
▶ **Molho de mancarra** – peanut sauce
▶ **Polvo** – octopus
▶ **Pudim de coco** – coconut pudding
▶ **Pudim de queijo** – pudding made with goat's milk cheese
▶ **Queijo de cabra** – goat's milk cream cheese
▶ **Xerém** – maize porridge served with various accompaniments

own farm. The increasing use of frozen foods on the islands is a questionable matter (and can even be dangerous) as there is little guarantee that there has been an unbroken cold chain in Cape Verde. You should also be wary of pork as there is no trichinella inspection programme, or anything similar, on some of the islands. Beef is usually not a problem but it is often quite tough. The most common side dishes served to accompany the fish and meat dishes are root vegetables such as sweet potatoes, carrots, manioc and yams, the cooked fruit of the breadfruit tree, cabbage and potatoes. Rice and chips are often served as well.

For dessert a pudding is often on the menu: *pudim de leite* (milk), *coco* (coconut) or *café* (coffee), as well as fresh fruit. Papayas and bananas are harvested throughout the year while mangos, guavas, *pinha* (custard apple), passion fruit, coconuts, apples, as well as pomegranates, figs and quinces from Fogo, are only available in season. The best known dessert is *doce de papaya com queijo* – candied slices of papaya with spicy goat's cheese. The goat's cheese from Fogo and Santo Antão is renowned in Cape Verde for its fine taste and good quality.

The continental breakfast *(kebra-djum-djum)* served in the smaller hotels and guesthouses usually consist of bread rolls, cheese, papaya jelly, fresh papaya, coffee and an orange juice. Most of the large hotels provide a substantial breakfast buffet. The coffee *(kafé)* from Fogo, as well as the wine grown on the island *(vinho de Fogo)* has a unique taste because the volcanic soil gives the beans and grapes a full, fruity flavour. Wine is not grown commercially on any other island but coffee is and you see the bushes with their bright red berries on Santo Antão and Santiago. All of the mountainous Cape Verde Islands produce the traditional island drink of *grogue* (sugar cane spirits). A dash of sugar cane syrup turns *grogue* into *pontche*, the traditional sugar cane liqueur. However, other liqueurs prepared with fruits, herbs or coconuts are also often called *pontche*.

Strela, the local beer *(serveja)*, is brewed in Praia the capital city. Beer (Sagres, Superbock) and wine imported from Portugal, as well as soft drinks from Europe and Brazil, are available almost everywhere while local mango and guava juice are particularly tasty. Bottled water *(águ)*, both local and Portuguese is also readily available and, if you want to stay healthy, you should stick to it: do not drink any tap water on Cape Verde!

There are plenty of local restaurants that serve simple, regional food. A *cachupa* is a standard dish in most of them and this is a good sign because it means that the locals eat there! It is a good idea to ask for INSIDER TIP the dish of the day *(prato do dia)* at lunchtime – it is always freshly prepared and usually very inexpensive. Stews, fish and chicken are the most common dishes.

Authentic regional cuisine is available in the smaller restaurants

Stalls at the side of road frequently offer small fried patties, grilled chicken legs and similar fare. As a rule you should only eat cooked foods and should avoid ice cubes and ice cream on all of the Cape Verde Islands.

Most restaurants are open from midday to 3pm and from 6/7pm to 10/11pm. Cafés are usually open all day long. You might go unnoticed if you sit down at an outside table so to avoid waiting too long it is best to go inside to place your order.

SHOPPING

Shopping in Cape Verde means visiting the local markets, they are the central point of the social life of every village and town. Half of the people living in the area there come together in the morning to do their shopping and exchange the latest news. The largest markets are on Santiago: there is not only a vibrant fruit and vegetable market in Praia but also a huge market selling household goods *(sucupira)*. It is only surpassed by the weekly market in Assomada *(Wed, Sat)*. At the markets you should keep an eye out for typical Cape Verde products because the local ceramics and traditional woven wickerwork items are sometimes difficult to spot among all of the glittery stuff from the Far East. Don't be misled into thinking that the African souvenirs that are now being sold everywhere are original Cape Verde products – they have absolutely nothing to do with Cape Verde.

all markets. The elaborately decorated vases with figural or geographic patterns are harder to find. The islands of Boavista, Sal, Maio, São Vicente and Santiago are all well known for their pottery.

GROGUE & PONTCHE

Typical Cape Verde souvenirs include *grogue*, the sugar cane liquor and *pontche*, the sweet liqueur. INSIDER TIP It is common for these drinks to be brewed privately, especially on the mountainous islands. Semicircular kilns next to the houses are a sign that *grogue* is produced there. The producers need a state licence but the quality of the produce is based on the experience of the producer. If you want to be sure that it is pure, only buy reputable liquor such as the brands available in supermarkets or from Alfred Mandl on Santo Antão

CERAMICS

Household items such as the large, bulbous water pots *(pote)* and dishes of unglazed clay for everyday use can be found at almost

MUSIC CDS & INSTRUMENTS

Music is the lifeblood of the Cape Verdeans and it is what they need to face up to the

Made in Cape Verde: traditional souvenirs that will bring back memories of your Cape Verde holiday after you return home

hardships of their existence and the good thing is that Cape Verdean music also acts as a balance to everyday stress for the tourists! Take a little bit of the Creole attitude towards life back home with you in the form of the typical sounds and rhythms of the islands' music. However, it is not easy to get an overview of all the different musical styles and musicians so it is best to find a shop that can give you expert advice. If you are musically inclined, you might like to try an original Cape Verdean instrument such as a drum, guitar or the small four-string *cavaquinho*. The luthier Luís Baptista and his brothers on São Vicente keep up the tradition of making stringed instruments. INSIDER TIP You will be able to see how a guitar, *rabeca* (violin) or *cavaquinho* is made if you visit their workshop in *Mindelo (tel. 9 92 66 92)*. The brothers are all musicians – maybe they tell you where the next gig is taking place ...

PANOS

Panos are narrow woven strips of cotton that are usually worn around the hips or as a strap for carrying babies. Traditional black and white fabrics with geometric patterns are made on Santiago and Fogo. There are modern variants in other colours and fibres. You will also find small bags and other accessories made out of *panos*.

VINHO DE FOGO

Volcanic ash gives the grapes their unique taste and Chã wine from the island of Fogo is a very special tipple. Distinctively aromatic wines with delicate nuances are pressed from the *moscatel branca* and *touriga nacional* grapes in the wine cooperative in Chã das Caldeiras. *Vinho de Fogo* can be purchased in many *mini mercados* and from the cooperative on Fogo.

THE PERFECT ROUTE

WHITE BEACH AND DESERT SAND

The best thing to do after you arrive at Boavista is to relax a bit on the fine sand beach of ❶ *Sal Rei* → p. 42. A sundowner in the Tortuga Beach Club or dinner at the Blu Marlin are perfect ways to end the day. On the next day, a trip to the ❷ *Deserto de Viana* → p. 43 will give you the real feeling of being in a desert. Then take off for Santiago from the airport near ❸ *Rabil* → p. 43.

PEOPLE AND HISTORY

Stroll through the country's capital of ❹ *Praia* → p. 57 with its lively vegetable market and the pedestrian precinct with cafés and a museum. ❺ *Cidade Velha* → p. 57, where famous seafarers and pirates went on land, is only 15km/9.3mi to the west. End the day at the Quinta da Montanha mountain lodge in Rui Vaz, from where you will have a magnificent panoramic view. Your trip around the island starts the next morning and takes you first to ❻ *Assomada* → p. 56, where there is plenty of hustle and bustle on market days (Wed and Sat) and then take a break for a picnic in the ❼ *Serra Malagueta Nature Reserve* → p. 59. A brief stop for a swim at ❽ *Tarrafal* → p. 59 will refresh you again before you head off along the rocky west coast to Praia to board the plane for Fogo.

VOLCANO AND WINE

You land in the picturesque capital ❾ *São Filipe* → p. 67. Take a taxi or get into a shared one (departure from the *mercado municipal*) and head up to the fascinating volcanic landscape of ❿ *Chã das Caldeiras* → p. 64 at an altitude of 1700m/5577ft where you can admire the colossal cone of the highest mountain in Cape Verde and the crater that erupted in 1995. Ramiro's Bar is the place to enjoy live music and a glass or two of Chã wine. But beware: only those who are very fit will be able to climb the ⓫ *Pico do Fogo* → p. 66 on the following morning (photo above)! You can then decide whether to stay another night before going back to São Filipe and then flying to São Vicente after a stopover in Praia.

JOIE DE VIVRE AND MUSIC

⓬ *Mindelo* → p. 78, the vibrant cultural capital of Cape Verde (photo right) is a place of fascinating contrasts. Magnificent colonial

architecture next to dilapidated buildings, elegant yachts in the marina and the homeless who have to sleep on the street – but you will feel joie de vivre wherever you go. A *noite caboverdeana* is a must before you set sail on the morning ferry to Santo Antão.

PASS ROADS AND PATHS ALONG THE CLIFFS

The old pass road from ⑬ *Porto Novo* → p. 88 leads at an altitude of 1400m/4593ft past the ⑭ *Cova Crater* → p. 89 up to Delgadim lookout point. It then continues on to ⑮ *Ribeira Grande* → p. 88 and along the coast to ⑯ *Ponta do Sol* → p. 87. Travel to Cruzinha in the morning and hike along the coast of Corvo and Fontainhas back to Ponta do Sol. On the next day, make a trip into the ⑰ *Ribeira do Paúl* → p. 88 high up to the Cabo da Ribeira. Make your way down to ⑱ *Vila das Pombas* → p. 89 and from there take a shared taxi back to Ribeira Grande and then on to Ponta do Sol. On the following day take a shared taxi to Porto Novo and then the ferry back to São Vicente.

SEA BREEZE AND ROARING WAVES

The beach hotel Foya Branca is located near the fishing village of ⑲ *São Pedro* → p. 80. You should not miss out on a walk along the beach and the excellent food in the Santo Andrée restaurant (opposite the hotel). Your plane then takes off from the nearby airport and you fly directly to Boavista or via Sal.

1200km/745mi
Pure travel time: 25 hours
Recommended duration: 2 weeks
Detailed map of the route on the back cover, in the road atlas and the pull-out map

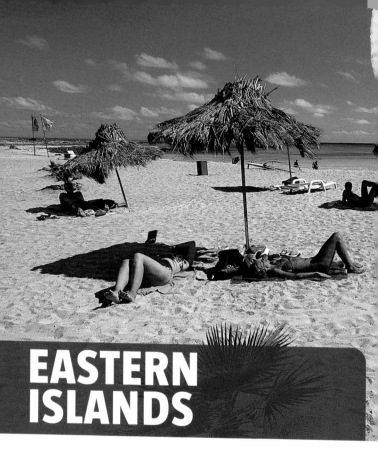

EASTERN ISLANDS

The air is dusty and dry, the fine sand blows into your ears and eyes – the three islands of Sal, Boavista and Maio are known as the 'desert islands' and the name suits them to a tee.

There is plenty of desert here – endless reddish brown fields of stone without any vegetation, where the occasional acacia bush rises from the barren soil – and dazzling white dunes formed from sand carried here from the Sahara. They all have some things in common: dust, shimmering heat and an almost surreal atmosphere. Once you have seen a mirage in this seemingly hostile landscape, you will feel that anything is possible.

It is amazing to see how the dry steppes and barren salt marshes gradually turn into the most wonderful beaches at the coast – miles of fine white sandy beaches and dazzling, crystal clear turquoise water that will fulfil all of your holiday dreams. The eastern islands are especially popular with water sports enthusiasts – the islands have the perfect conditions for wind and kite surfing, surfing, sailing, diving, snorkelling and fishing.

Ornithologists and other nature lovers will also find plenty to interest them on the desert islands as they can observe ospreys and tropical sea birds as well as the sea turtles that come on shore on

Photo: Praia de Santa Maria on Sal

Endless, white beaches, turquoise ocean and shady desert oases: welcome to a paradise for water sports enthusiasts!

peaceful summer nights to dig out a nest and lay their eggs in the warm sand.

From around the year 1620 the salt trade played an important role on Sal and Boavista, and influenced the lives of the people living there more than on any other Cape Verdean island. It assured work and prosperity for 200 years and made the eastern islands the most important and wealthiest in the archipelago.

Volcanic activity ceased much earlier on the eastern islands than on the others and soil erosion wore down the rock – except for a few volcanic craters and monadnocks – and created the flat, desert-like surface. The wind carries fine sand from the Sahara across the Atlantic that, together with the weathered sedimentary stones, creates fine sandy beaches along the coast.

Wellness in a volcanic crater: a dip in the salt pans at Pedra de Lume

SAL

(134 B–C 2–5) (∅ Q–R 4–6) **30km/ 18.5mi from north to south, 12km/7.5mi from west to east: Sal (pop. 26,000) is the most north-eastern island in the archipelago and the flattest of all.**

Its highest elevations are *Monte Leste* (263m/863ft) and *Monte Grande* (406m/ 1332ft). Both are part of a volcanic chain in the rugged terrain in the north of the island. Just a few dozen people live here; the only signs of life are a few solitary goats wandering freely across the stony fields. The barrenness of the landscape is only relieved by a few withered acacias and a small amount of farming in the area around Terra Boa. Tourists find the Buracona rock formation and the salt works near Pedra de Lume to the north of the island's capital Espargos interesting. Travelling south, the fields of stone gradually turn into a landscape of low dunes and finally into miles of picture-perfect fine sandy beaches. This is where you will find the Cape Verde tourist flag-ship of Santa Maria. What was once an insider's tip in the 1970s has now become well known worldwide yet it has man-aged to remain rather peaceful. Water sports enthusiasts say that the wind here is even better than the beautiful beaches. The strong trade winds are a delight for surfers and yachtsmen from November to June – swimmers are usually less en-thusiastic. You will encounter the true nature of the Cape Verdean lifestyle in the island's capital of Espargos which is just over a mile away from the international airport.

SIGHTSEEING

BURACONA (134 B3) *(∅ Q4)*
In Buracona, on the north-west coast, you will be able to admire the *Olho Azul,* a deep hole in the volcanic rock. The seawater glitters in a spectacular blue when the sun hits it from the right angle **INSIDER TIP** (approx. 11am–1pm). There are natural swimming pools where you can take a dip not far away. Take the coastal road from Palmeira to the north: approx. 6km/3.7mi.

yellow and pink look quite European until you spot the colourfully dressed women selling bananas, papayas and freshly caught fish in bright plastic bowls on the side of the road. European? African? A bit of everything. The men gather to play *oril* under shady trees while the Praça 5 de Julho in the centre of the village appears drowsy. That is where you can visit the turquoise *Nazarene church* and most of the town's guesthouses and restaurants are also nearby.

ESPARGOS (134 B3) (*ฎ R5*)

The island's capital city (pop. 17,000) at the foot of ≥✫ *Monte Curral* is not very spectacular but there is a lovely panoramic view over the northern part of the island from the mountain top. The cube shaped one and two storey houses in shades of blue,

PALMEIRA (134 B3) (*ฎ R5*)

The former fishing village of Palmeira (pop. 1400) has become the main hub for everything that reaches the island by ship. Oil tankers and container ships unload their cargo here. The up-and-coming harbour town is becoming increasingly important for the island and not much remains of what was once a picturesque port village.

PEDRA DE LUME ★ (134 B3) (*ฎ R5*)

The ● *salt works* near the hamlet of Pedra de Lume (pop. 330) are only a few miles

---

★ Pedra de Lume
Swimmers can only float in the buoyant salt pan waters → p. 35

★ Praia de Santa Maria
Crystal clear turquoise water and white sand → p. 39

★ Deserto de Viana
An endless chain of dunes – all the way to the horizon → p. 43

★ Sal Rei
Once a drowsy fishing village, Boavista's capital is being transformed into a holiday resort → p. 44

★ Wreck of the Cabo de Santa Maria
Bizarre skeleton of a cargo ship that ran aground 40 years ago → p. 44

★ Praia de Santa Mónica
Endless expanse: a deserted and pristine beach that is not very easy to reach → p. 46

★ Vila do Maio
Time moves at a slower pace in Maio's small capital → p. 50

★ Praia de Santana
25m/82ft high dunes of fine Sahara sand → p. 52

MARCO POLO HIGHLIGHTS

away from Espargos. Salt production was once the economic engine of the entire island. A natural crater, with its base below sea level, offered perfect conditions for the salt trade. A tunnel was bored through the crater wall and later a cable car was used to transport salt to the port.

restored *weighing house* and some ancient wooden *windmills* on the Praça Marcelo Leitão and in front of the Hotel Morabeza bear witnesses to this period. Nowadays, tourism has become the most important economic factor and there are more and more hotels and holiday resorts springing

You can shop for souvenirs in the pretty colonial houses on Rua 1 de Junho

The salt works lost their importance at the end of the 19th century. Today, only a handful of fishermen live in Pedra de Lume and the salt works are only a tourist attraction. Take a INSIDER TIP dip in one of the salt pans – it is the same as in the Dead Sea; you cannot sink *(daily 7am– 6pm | entrance fee 500 CVE)*. The café *(open daily)* serves cold drinks and sandwiches and there are showers and deckchairs to relax in.

SANTA MARIA (134 B5) *(ᗜ R6)*
Santa Maria is another small town (pop. 6300) that owes its existence to salt. The

up – private investments and construction projects are booming. Most holidaymakers stay in the hotel district to the west of the old harbour quay that runs for a few miles along the beach. There are beach clubs run by the hotels, restaurants, surf stations and diving schools along the entire length of the beach promenade. During the day, there is plenty of action here but the downtown area is more interesting in the evening: countless souvenir shops, bars and restaurants provide entertainment for all tastes.

The town centre consists of the main square, the Praça Marcelo Leitão, with the

Catholic church and the three adjacent parallel streets Rua Amílcar Cabral, Rua 1 de Junho and Rua 15 de Agosto. The one and two storey houses in various stages of dilapidation and a few manor houses in the Portuguese colonial style form a fascinating contrast to the modern shops.

FOOD & DRINK

There is only a choice of cafés and restaurants in Santa Maria and Espargos, the smaller villages have very little on offer.

D'ANGELA
This restaurant is almost unrivalled, it serves excellent, inexpensive food and is right by the sea! If you want, you can sit at a table on the sand and watch all the action around you. The fish dishes are especially tasty. INSIDER TIP Fridays barbecue evening and usually live music. *Daily | Santa Maria | Rua Indepedencia | tel. 2 42 13 62 | Budget–Moderate*

AMÉRICO'S
A good option – Cape Verde and international cuisine that is always deliciously prepared. The most pleasant place to sit is upstairs on the airy, shady terrace. *Fri–Wed | Santa Maria | Rua 1 de Junho | tel. 2 42 10 11 | Moderate*

ATLANTIS
Cosy ambience with a view of the Atlantic along with select wines and fine French Creole cuisine. The attractive architecture makes its greatest impression in the evening. INSIDER TIP Reasonably priced lunchtime specials. *Daily | Santa Maria | beach promenade (opposite the Hotel Belorizonte) | tel. 2 42 18 79 | Moderate*

COMPAD
Authentic Cape Verde cuisine that is a rarity in Santa Maria. Delicious food, friendly service and reasonable prices. Daily lunchtime specials. *Daily | Santa Maria | Rua 1 de Junho | Budget*

CAFÉ CULTURAL
There is often a lot of hustle and bustle in this café right on the busy main square. Cool drinks, Creole cuisine or a snack with pleasant music – what more could one want? Maybe an exotic cocktail or freshly squeezed fruit juice? *Daily | Santa Maria | Praça Marcelo Leitão | tel. 2 42 21 54 | Budget*

PASTELARIA DADÓ
This café serves cakes and sandwiches from its own bakery and very economical main dishes. You can buy the magnificently fragrant *pao de coco* (coconut cake) fresh from the tray in the shop next door. *Daily | Santa Maria | Rua 15 de Agosto | Budget*

INSIDER TIP O FAROLIM
The restaurant in the Hotel Odjo d'Água has a really magical location above the sea. The sound of the surf, Cape Verde songs and an exquisite meal – the most beautiful place on the island for a romantic dinner. Not exclusively for hotel guests! *Daily | Santa Maria | in the Odjo d'Água hotel complex | tel. 2 42 14 14 | Moderate*

ZUM FISCHERMANN
Run by German expats who are real experts in preparing fish. Not only do they serve fantastic dishes but they can also answer any questions you might have on the subject. The restaurant is decorated with some magnificent shells and shell pictures. *Daily | Santa Maria | opposite the BCA bank | tel. 9 91 76 00 | Moderate*

RISTORANTE LEONARDO
Fine Italian delicacies in friendly surroundings. Alessandro the proprietor serves tasty meat dishes, fresh fish, homemade pasta and a superb selection of international

wines. *Daily | Santa Maria | centre | tel. 9 81 00 57 | Expensive*

MANLULELE
Italian Cape Verde cuisine that is authentic and inexpensive: sandwiches, daily specials and delicacies such as kid *(cabrito)*. Often with live music in the evening. *Wed–Mon | Santa Maria | Rua 1 de Junho | tel. 2 42 21 65 | Budget*

CHEZ PASTIS
Not cheap, but exquisite – the chef is a real master of his art! The fish and seafood are particularly outstanding. Reservations are essential as there are only four tables! *Daily | Santa Maria | Rua Amílcar Cabral | tel. 9 84 36 96 | Expensive*

SALINAS
Local and Portuguese cuisine, as well as delicious authentic Italian pizzas. *Daily | Espargos | Rua 5 de Julho | tel. 2 41 23 18 | Budget*

SHOPPING

There are just as many souvenir shops as there are restaurants and cafés in the centre of *Santa Maria*. Most of them sell arts and crafts from Africa: batik clothes, paintings, sculptures, jewellery and much more. There is a similar selection of wares in the *old vegetable market building* on Rua Amílcar Cabral. This is where there is the greatest variety and competition between the traders – and also where the traders are particularly insistent on you making a purchase.

ART LOJA CAB VERD
Arts and crafts from the Cape Verde Islands – jewellery, bags, t-shirts, souvenirs made of coconut and metal, wine, coffee, salt etc. *Also open Sun | Espargos | Rua de Bom Dia*

TROPICAL DANCE
This establishment has a wide selection of items, good advice, a great deal of dedication. *Espargos | Rua 5 de Julho*

SPORTS & ACTIVITIES

For experienced surfers the best surfing areas lie in the south-west *(Ponta Preta)* and south-east *(Praia da Fragata)* of the island; beginners should stay in the bay between the *Ponta de Leme Bedje* and the *Ponta do Sinó*. There are several bases for wind and kite surfing, as well as board surfing, at the *Praia de Santa Maria* and *Praia Leme Bedje* (134 B5) *(⫘ R6)*. They rent out equipment and organise various courses.

The *Orca Dive Club (Santa Maria | tel. 2 42 13 02 | www.orca-diveclub-caboverde. com)* runs several courses and dive trips around the island, such as to the Olho Azul. Boat excursions include the *Neptunus* (boat with an underwater observation cabin), trips to sunken shipwrecks and to admire the marine life; *Praia de Santa Maria | tel. 9 88 71 07)* and the *Trimaran (reservations one day in advance at the quayside, daily 10.30am–1pm, or in the Hotel Morabeza | Praia de Santa Maria)*. The latter also does day trips to Boavista that include a tour of the island and lunch. If you want to explore the island on two wheels, you can hire mountain bikes and motor scooters from *Bebe Beach Rent (in front of the Hotel Morabeza | Santa Maria | tel. 9 70 13 03)*.

BEACHES

A chain of perfect beaches starts at *Praia de Santa Maria* and makes its way as far as *Baía de Algodoeiro*. However, there is no shade at all and only umbrellas at those places that cater to tourists. If you want to spread out your beach towel anywhere else, make sure you have everything – from sunburn protection to bottles of water – with you.

BAÍA DE ALGODOEIRO
(134 B4) *(∭ R6)*

A path leading to the beaches on the west coast starts about 4km/2.5mi to the north of Santa Maria in the direction of Espargos. Things are still rather peaceful here but there are plans for the island's new holiday centres to be set up in the vicinity and there is a lot of building activity.

BAÍA DE MURDEIRA
(134 B4) *(∭ R5)*

Murdeira is on the west coast around 6km/3.7mi south of Espargos. There is a smaller cove in the long bay and it is absolutely ideal for bathing! A holiday complex with apartments and restaurants provides the perfect infrastructure for a beach break; also for day guests.

COSTA DA FRAGATA
(134 B4–5) *(∭ R6)*

A desert track leads about 3km/1.8mi north of Santa Maria to the Costa da Fragata on the south-east coast. The 4km/2.5mi long beach is not particularly wide but it is very popular with kite surfers.

PONTA PRETA (134 B5) *(∭ R6)*

The rocky promontory of Ponta Preta is around 2km/1.2mi from Santa Maria. Several windsurfing world championships have made it famous but this popular surf spot is only suitable for real experts!

PRAIA DE SANTA MARIA ★
(134 B5) *(∭ R6)*

The main beach of the island stretches 9km/5.6mi from the Ponta do Sinó to the Ponta Preta. The hotels, beach bars and clubs create a holiday atmosphere and there are surf and diving bases that offer all kinds of water sports.

The Praia de Santa Maria is a paradise for windsurfers

Just relax and enjoy: under a sunshade at the Hotel Morabeza's beach club

ENTERTAINMENT

Those who want hustle and bustle in the evening will find what they are looking for in *Santa Maria*. There are any number of pubs, bars and discos on *Rua 1 de Junho* and on the adjacent streets and you can be sure to find live music somewhere.

BLU BAR
Cosy, unpretentious pub with great cocktails and excellent live music/jam sessions. *Daily | behind the church*

CALEMA PUB
The feel-good bar: their cool cocktails draw in the young surfer crowd. Almost always live music. *Daily*

CHILL OUT CAFÉ
The international meeting place! Guests from all over the world come here to have fun or watch sports programmes. With internet access (very expensive). *Daily*

OCEAN CAFÉ
This is the perfect place for those who like it chic and stylish, and it seems like many do, it is always packed in the evening ... *Daily | Praça Marcelo Leitão*

PIRATA CLUB
The pirate-style disco comes complete with the Jolly Roger and all the trappings. *Sat from 11pm | on the way into town*

WHERE TO STAY

LES ALIZÉS
Ten cheerful rooms in a prettily renovated old colonial house. Family atmosphere. Breakfast is served on the ☆ rooftop terrace with a view of the ocean. *Santa Maria | Rua 1 de Junho | tel. 2 42 14 46 | www.pensao-les-alizes.com | Moderate*

HOTEL ATLÂNTICO
Right at the village entrance and especially suitable for tourists passing through.

54 recently renovated rooms with bathroom and air conditioning. *Espargos | Rua Amílcar Cabral | tel. 2 41 12 10 | hotel atlantico@cvtelecom.cv | Moderate*

HOTEL DUNAS DE SAL
Modern four star designer hotel with a great deal of light and minimalist interiors. In a quiet location right on the beach. Two swimming pools, spa, gym and dive centre. Santa Maria is a 20 minute walk away. *48 rooms | Ponta Preta | tel. 2 42 90 50 | www.hoteldunasdesal.com | Expensive*

HOTEL DA LUZ
Reasonably priced, pleasant family hotel on the outskirts of the town centre, with swimming pool in the courtyard. 38 basic rooms with air conditioning, just ten minutes away from the centre of town. *Santa Maria | tel. 2 42 11 38 | Budget*

HOTEL MORABEZA
The best hotel in town: a prestigious four star hotel right on the beach with three restaurants, family suites, mini-golf, various excursion and leisure activities. Tasteful ambience, spacious rooms. Karaoke on Friday in the bar and those who take part get a caipirinha. *140 rooms | Praia de Santa Maria | tel. 2 42 10 20 | www.hotel morabeza.com | Expensive*

HOTEL ODJO D'ÁGUA
Four star hotel with a private beach, on a promontory right near the centre of town. The charmingly decorated rooms are located around a palm-fringed patio and almost all have a private terrace. Three restaurants, swimming pool, spa and gym. *46 rooms | Santa Maria | tel. 2 42 14 14 | www.odjodagua-hotel.com | Expensive*

PAZ E BEM
Guesthouse with 16 basic rooms run by Italian Franciscan nuns – well maintained with friendly staff. *Espargos | Rua Jorge Barbosa (near the Nazarene church) | tel. 2 411 7 82 | Budget*

PORTA DO VENTO
Rooms decorated according to feng shui principles with a comfortable, cosmopolitan atmosphere. Opened in 2006. *15 rooms| Santa Maria | on the outskirts of town | tel. 2 42 21 21 | www.porta dovento.com | Moderate*

INFORMATION

Information kiosk on the *Praça Marcelo Leitão* (Mon–Sat 10am–5pm) in *Santa Maria*. Information booklets, town maps, phone cards, international telephone calls.

LOW BUDGET

▶ Many of the bars and hotels in *Santa Maria* have a happy hour in the afternoon or early evening and drinks are as much as 50 per cent cheaper. There are various times and these can change so look for their notice signs. One of the nicest places for an inexpensive happy hour is the terrace of the *Tortuga Beach Club* in the Hotel Morabeza with a view of the sea.

▶ You can save money wherever you find a *casa de pasto* sign. These are inns – often tiny – where the locals enjoy food that is freshly prepared every day. There is no menu and there are often only one or two dishes – possibly a *catchupa* or another kind of stew or a special of the day with fish or chicken. And you will be able to rub shoulders with the Cape Verdeans!

BOAVISTA

(135 D–F 2–5) (🗺 R–S 8–10) **The name Boavista means 'beautiful view' as well as 'beautiful sight'. And today tourists have the island in their sights when they plan their beach and water sports holiday: the island offers the ideal conditions for surfing and diving.**

very much: the capital city Sal Rei found itself once again threatened by high sand drifts just a few years later.

It comes as no surprise that, with its extreme environmental and climatic conditions, Boavista once had the lowest population in the archipelago. Today, around 8700 people live here, about two thirds of them in the capital of Sal Rei. The name Sal Rei (royal salt) explains why a settle-

A Cape Verdean fisherman applying new coat of paint

The third largest of the Cape Verde Islands boasts 55km/34mi of beach. White dunes of powdery white sand, reddish brown lunar landscapes and secluded oases of palm trees are its additional highlights. It is said that Boavista is the Sahara of the Cape Verdes. The wind carries in fine sand from the Sahara and the sand forms gigantic shifting dunes that gradually make their way over the island. Walls were even built in 1915/16 to protect the island from the shifting sand but they did not help

ment was founded on this barren island in the 17th century: salt of the finest quality. Trading with the 'white gold' was synonymous with wealth and prosperity. Boavista was the most important island in the archipelago for a number of years. However, the island suffered setbacks – plundered by pirates, catastrophic periods of drought and famine – and a decline in the salt trade meant a slide back into insignificance. A handful of colonial houses in Sal Rei bring back memories of its glory days. Tourism promises a golden future and along with Sal, Boavista is the second island that wants to attract tourists with all-inclusive offers in hotels with several thousand beds.

SIGHTSEEING

DESERTO DE VIANA ⭐
(135 E3) (*𝄞 R9*)
The only large sandy desert in Cape Verde stretches from Estancia de Baixo for a few miles to the north-east. Hills and valleys of fine sand undulate in front of a chain of hills as far the eye can see. It really does real like the desert: the incessant wind will blow away your tracks in the sand and some people even see things that are not there. A mirage!

FÁBRICA DA CHAVE (135 D3) (*𝄞 R9*)
The historic brickworks and its outbuildings have been almost completely swallowed by the sand. But you will still be able to find it if you walk to the south along the beach from Sal Rei. A clearly visible chimney shows you the way. The walk takes around one hour and leads through fields of dunes and a lagoon that form part of a nature reserve. With a little bit of luck, you might even be able to spot some rare birds.

POVOAÇÃO VELHA
(135 D4) (*𝄞 R10*)
The oldest settlement on Boavista (pop. 300) is in the south of the island. Povoação Velha is a tiny village but there is often plenty of activity. There is a café on the main square and the charming *Nossa Senhora da Conceição* church (built in 1828) is perched on a little hill above the village. It is only about 15km/9.3mi from Rabil in the direction of Praia de Santa Mónica but you will need an off-road vehicle for the trip.

RABIL (135 D3) (*𝄞 R9*)
Today, the old capital (pop. 1200) of the island appears rather slow-moving. The oldest church on Boavista, the *Igreja São Roque,* as well as a *pottery school (Escola de Olaria)*, can be found in the village. The traditional art of pottery making is taught in the school but it is usually closed – however, if you should happen to meet somebody there, you will be able to look around a bit.

TURTLES IN DANGER

Sea turtles have lived on our planet for around 225 million years. They survived ice ages and saw how mammals – and finally, man – developed. Today these living fossils are threatened with extinction. Although it is strictly forbidden, there is still a market for turtle meat, eggs and tortoiseshell. Environmental pollution, as well as the destruction of nesting beaches and construction in their vicinity, is playing a detrimental role and many animals also end up in trawl nets.
You can help protect these fascinating creatures: never buy any tortoiseshell souvenirs, pay attention to the protective measures at the nesting beaches and give vent to your annoyance if anybody tries to sell you turtle products. Further information at *www.sostartarugas.org* and *www.turtle-foundation.org*.

SAL REI ⭐ (135 D3) (*🛈 R9*)

Boavista's capital is the only town of any size on the island (pop. 5800). The Avenida dos Emigrantes runs from the airport to the town and you just have to go around the corner and you are in the centre of town the *Praça Santa Isabel*. The first thing you will notice is the Catholic

The Cape Verdean fishing industry and international tourist operations are separated by the old port pier. The once rather drowsy hotel and leisure district *Praia de Estoril* is now developing rapidly to the south. Many new restaurants and guesthouses are also being opened in the town.

The wreck of the Cabo de Santa Maria off the north coast has now broken apart

church with its yellow and blue façade framed by two towers on the right and a few two storey colonial houses and the new market hall on the left. Things are livelier in the *fishing district* where a row of tiny yellow, pink, turquoise and green cottages line the *Avenida dos Pescadores*. The doors are open, the people living there relax in the shade along the pavement, dogs doze and children quarrel. Life here seems to be almost completely untouched by tourism. Women sit in the shade of the acacia trees at the beach and gut fish and children play in the sand next to the colourful fishing boats.

WRECK OF THE CABO DE SANTA MARIA ⭐ (135 E2) (*🛈 R8*)

The rusted wreck of the Spanish cargo ship the Cabo de Santa Maria lies on the Costa de Boa Esperança, 8km/5mi northwest of Sal Rei. The bizarre wreck is very close to the beach and is a great photo opportunity. Unfortunately there have been frequent muggings there in the past and you should definitely not visit the wreck if you are alone! It can only be reached in an off-road vehicle over a tricky dirt road from the Praia da Chave to the north. It is a good idea to use the services of a local driver for this trip.

FOOD & DRINK

BAR BIA
Nondescript but worth a visit: specialises in grilled food (you should order in advance). Ask what the special of the day is! **INSIDER TIP** Be adventurous and try their moray eel. *Mon–Sat | Sal Rei | Av. Amílcar Cabral | tel. 2 51 13 40 | Budget*

BLU MARLIN
A tiny restaurant with Italian Creole cooking that outshines all the others. Make sure to make a reservation; there are only four tables! Also breakfast, sandwiches and cakes. *Mon–Sat | Sal Rei | Praça Santa Isabel (two houses next to the market hall) | tel. 2 51 10 99 | Budget*

INSIDER TIP CAFÉ CANTA MORNA
The stylish ambience is a balm for the spirit while the fine Italian coffee and fresh, homemade cake are perfect for the body! *Daily | Sal Rei | Av. Amílcar Cabral | tel. 2 51 11 43 | Budget*

NAIDA
Donna Naida is a celebrity in Sal Rei and her excellent food is just as famous. That is why you should reserve in advance. *Daily | Sal Rei | Praça Santa Isabel | tel. 2 51 11 73 | Budget*

ROSY
Traditional home-style cooking in all its variants: fish, meat, chicken, squid, seafood. Generous portions that are very good. Try to order 2 hours in advance. *Mon–Sat | Sal Rei | Av. Amílcar Cabral | tel. 2 51 12 42 | Budget*

SODADE DI NHA TERRA
Well-established, tucked away restaurant that serves excellent Cape Verdean cuisine. This is no surprise as Sr. Amando once worked abroad. Daily lunchtime specials. *Daily | Rabil | Av. Almeida Marques | tel. 2 51 10 48 | Budget*

SHOPPING

African arts and crafts are sold in several small souvenir shops around the *Praça Santa Isabel* in *Sal Rei* as well as on the top floor of the market hall. Some African dealers also sell their wares in a row of shops in front of the ● *Polivalente Sport Stadium,* on the old harbour quay where *oril* players also gather for a game or two.

DEUSA TERRA
Caterina, an Italian woman, crafts striking handmade **INSIDER TIP** jewellery out of silver and natural materials. *Sal Rei | Praça Santa Isabel | tel. 9 50 25 12*

SPORTS & ACTIVITIES

The *Praia de Estoril* is the in place for all kinds of water sports, for all levels of expertise. There are numerous surfing and diving bases, such as the *Submarine Center, Happy Surfpool, Boavista Wind Club (www.boavistawindclub.com).* Experienced surfers and pros will find great conditions in the south, north and especially in the east: *Praia de Cabral (135 D3) (ﾉ R9), Praia da Antónia (135 E2) (ﾉ R–S8)* and *Praia das Gatas (135 F3) (ﾉ S9).* Beginners should stay in the *bay at Sal Rei* as it is protected by a barrier island just off the coast. Excursions on Boavista always head for the desert. The more adventurous can hire an off-road vehicle; those who are not so courageous can either take a car with a local driver who knows his way around (the hotel reception can help arrange this) or participate in a tour in an *aluguer*. *Baobab Tours (Rabil | tel. 2 51 11 11)* can give you an insider's view of life on Boavista. Franca and Ralf show visitors aspects of Cape Verde that they would not discover by themselves. Their offers include some easy trekking excursions with a pickup to 'Sal Rei by Night'. You can book catamaran excursions at the old harbour quay *(tel. 9 92 95 92)*.

BEACHES

Boavista has the longest and most beautiful beaches of the Cape Verde Islands. The fine white Sahara sand and the crystal clear turquoise water are incomparable; the constant north-east trade wind is perfect for surfers. A bottle of water, sunscreen and a hat are all absolutely essential!

PRAIA DA CHAVE
(135 D3) (*📍 R9*)
A beach that stretches for miles with high sand dunes. However, this picture-perfect beach has attracted investors and several hotel complexes with accommodation for thousands of holidaymakers are planned for the future.

PRAIA DO CURRALINHO
(135 D4) (*📍 R10*)
The continuation of the Praia de Santa Mónica, it is often too windy for swimming but ideal for a walk along the beach.

PRAIA DE ESTORIL
(135 D3) (*📍 R9*)
The Praia de Estoril stretches around 10km/6.2mi south from Sal Rei. It is perfect for water sports which makes it very popular. In addition to the surfing and diving bases, there are beach umbrellas, sun loungers, restaurants and cafés. The Ilha de Sal Rei off the coast protects the bay from wind and waves.

PRAIA DE SANTA MÓNICA ★
(135 D4) (*📍 R10*)
This powdery white sand beach seems to stretch forever – it is actually 18km/11.2mi long. It can only be reached in an off-road vehicle – preferably with a local driver or booked from one of the many organisations that offer this excursion for individual persons and groups.

PRAIA VARANDINHA
(135 D4) (*📍 R9*)
The desert stretches down to the sea and the bizarre rock formations form an impressive backdrop, and a grotto provides shade. Extremely windy, but great for walks. There is a lighthouse on the limestone plateau at the westernmost point on Boavista, the Ponta Varandinha.

ENTERTAINMENT

There are regular live music performances in many of the bars and restaurants in the centre of *Sal Rei* and on weekends people let their hair down with the music and dancing at the *Praça Santa Isabel*.

BOAVISTA SOCIAL CLUB
Sit on the beach with a drink in hand and count the stars ... or just chat, listen to music and people watch ... or make new friends ... or dance in the disco on Friday night ... *Daily | Praia de Estoril*

MORABEZA
A hip beach establishment; popular with tourists and locals alike. Reggae night on Tuesdays. *Daily | Praia de Estoril*

INSIDER TIP ▶ TORTUGA BEACH CLUB
Expensive, but a great place for a sundowner. *Daily | Praia de Estoril*

WHERE TO STAY

HOTEL BOAVISTA
Well maintained modern establishment at the entrance to town. *34 rooms | Sal Rei |*

Av. 4 de Julho | tel. 2 511145 | hotelboavista @cvtelecom.cv | *Moderate*

HOTEL DUNAS

Well kept, Spanish run hotel in the centre of town with a wonderful terrace and private beach. *17 rooms | Sal Rei | Av. Amílcar Cabral | tel. 2 511225 | dunas. boavista@gmail.com* | *Expensive*

ESTORIL BEACH RESORT

22 spacious rooms and 23 apartments make up this modern hotel complex with a Moorish ambience, only a stone's throw away from the sea. *Praia de Estoril | tel. 2 511078 | www.estorilbeachresort.com* | *Moderate*

HOTEL MIGRANTE LODGE

Small, but especially elegant: four individually decorated rooms in a beautifully renovated colonial house with a leafy patio. In the centre of Sal Rei. *Sal Rei | Av. Amílcar Cabral | tel. 2 511143 | www.migrante-guesthouse.com* | *Expensive*

APARTHOTEL CA' NICOLA

Generously sized, well equipped apartments with private terraces around a beautiful courtyard where the social life takes place – breakfast, bar, reception, bookshelves. Ideal for families. Under Italian management, right on the beach. *Sal Rei | tel. 2 511793 | www.canicola. com* | *Expensive*

INSIDER TIP ORQUIDEA

A place where you will feel at home: ten rooms with tasteful furniture, each with a private balcony (complete with hammock) around a magnificent, shady patio full of greenery. There are some colourful parrots and several friendly dogs that belong to the family. Close to the beach. *Sal Rei | tel. 2 511041 | www.guesthouse orquidea.com* | *Moderate*

A stroll along the Praia Varandinha is ideal for those looking for peace and quiet

Guests of the Hotel Parque das Dunas have the beautiful Praia da Chave beach at their doorstep

HOTEL PARQUE DAS DUNAS

Comfortable holiday resort right on the Praia da Chave, south of Sal Rei. 28 apartments of various sizes with terrace in a garden with a swimming pool. Make sure to ask for an apartment with a sea view! *Praia da Chave | tel. 2 511 2 90 | www.parque dasdunas.com | Expensive*

SANTA ISABEL

This small guesthouse under friendly Cape Verdean management is located in the centre of Sal Rei. Very good value for money; clean and modern. *9 rooms | Sal Rei | Praça Santa Isabel | tel. 2 511 2 52 | Budget*

SPINGUERA ECOLODGE ● ☺

The Italian owner Nicola and his daughter have transformed an isolated hamlet into an oasis of peace and quiet. And they went all the way: no telephones, no internet and television, air conditioning and mobile phones are also taboo. The *Ca Cabra (Expensive)* restaurant serves excellent Cape Verdean Italian food prepared from fresh local produce. *14 units | Espingueira | tel. 2 511 9 41 | www.spinguera.com | Expensive*

WHERE TO GO

ILHA DE SAL REI ☼
(135 D3) *(ⓜ R9)*

The small island off the coast of Sal Rei played an important strategic role: in 1818, the *Fort Duque do Bragança* was built there to defend against pirates. The remains of the fortifications with its old canons can still be seen. Ask one of the fishermen at the beach to take you across in his boat. The view back to Sal Rei is spectacular.

MAIO

(137 E–F 1–3) (⚏ P–Q 14–16) **Silence reigns supreme on Maio where it is secluded and the nature has remained pristine. The smallest of the desert islands provides a refuge for both endangered animals such as the osprey and sea turtle as well as for stressed holidaymakers.**

Rest and relaxation are the treasures that Maio has to offer. The fact that little Maio was not able to keep up with its sister islands in terms of development and progress has become a great advantage, especially now that the basic infrastructure requirements have been fulfilled: electricity and telephone networks, improved education and health care, well paved roads and transport links to the rest of the archipelago. These changes have also drawn the attention of investors.

While the main objective on Sal and Boavista seems to be to earn as much from tourism as possible, they do things differently on Maio. Time and silence are two of the few valuable things the island has no shortage of. The material wealth Maio once possessed – salt – was siphoned off by Portuguese and English traders in the 18th and 19th centuries. The island saw some of this prosperity in the form of a few colonial houses, a Catholic church and a fortress. But, at the same time, the feudal system was strengthened: decades after the abolishment of slavery on the other islands, hundreds of slaves were still at their white masters' mercy on Maio. The island was characterised by poverty and despair. Many of the inhabitants perished in the frequent droughts and famines; others escaped by emigrating.

Today, around 7000 people live on Maio, the majority of them in the island's capital of Vila do Maio on the south-west coast. The remainder have their homes in small villages near the ring road which circles the island. In contrast to the other two desert islands, there are many trees on Maio and there are even extensive acacia forests as a result of the reforestation activities in the north and west, and there are groves of palm trees in the coastal areas. Despite this, most of the island (104mi²) is made up of sparsely covered steppe and parched salt marshes. A few undulating hills of weathered volcanic craters and limestone rocks rise up in the middle and south-east of the island; the highest point is Monte Penoso (436m/1430ft).

SIGHTSEEING

ACACIA FORESTS
No other Cape Verde island has such an extensively forested area. Reforestation efforts created two acacia forest that now cover an area of 8650 acres. They stretch from the road between Morro and Calheta to the east *(137 E3) (⚏ P15)* and between Cascabulho and Pedro Vaz to the north *(137 F2) (⚏ P–Q15)*. This area is also home to gigantic grasshoppers and guinea fowl that hide in the underbrush.

CALHETA *(137 E3) (⚏ P15)*
Calheta is the second largest town (pop. 1200) on the island. The small *church* on the main square has a sweeping white and yellow façade; visitors enter from the side chapel. There are a few examples of colonial architecture on the main street *Rua São José* and small low houses in pastel shades in the straight, partly unpaved side streets. Around 3km/1.8mi from Morro; 8km/5mi from Vila do Maio in a northerly direction.

MORRO *(137 E3) (⚏ P15)*
The little village of Morro (pop. 300) is located on both sides of the ring road, in

the midst of coconut palms. The local hand-work cooperative makes very attractive traditional pottery. It is only a short walk through the palm grove to a magnificent beach. The *Ribeira do Morro* valley is especially interesting for amateur archaeologists: this is where the INSIDER TIP oldest rocks in the archipelago were found. You can see the *Monte Batalha* (294m/8648ft) in the north-east. Around 5km/3mi north of Vila do Maio.

RIBEIRA DOM JOÃO
(137 F3) (*Q15–16*)
The Ribeira Dom João valley stretches in a green oasis from the plateau all the way down to the sea. A grove of palm trees on the outskirts of the village of the same name (pop. 200) stretches almost to the river mouth that flows to a wonderful beach with fine, white sand. Around 12km/7.5mi to the east of Vila do Maio (turn-off in Figueira Seca).

SALT WORKS
(137 E3) (*P15–16*)
The salt works start in Vila do Maio and continue for around 5km/3mi in a northerly direction. Plants that have adapted to the salt have become established in the glittering rosy pink and white hills of salt. They provide local and migratory birds with a suitable place to rest and feed.

Fruit and vegetable sellers are a common sight in Vila do Maio

VILA DO MAIO ★
(137 E3) (*P16*)
The capital of the island (pop. 3000) used to be known as Porto Inglês. It lies on a high plateau above the sea. The city centre is crowned by the white church *Nossa Senhora da Luz* the perches at the top of a broad flight of stairs. Its two massive towers flank the gabled front with its Baroque elements. There is also a bank and hotel, as well as some cafés and shops, on the park-like church square. The *Casa Cardoso*, a colonial house from the town's heyday, is only a short distance away. The wealthiest salt trader on the island had it built at the beginning of the 20th century.

There are many tiny cottages in the grid-style streets that lead to the harbour. They are painted in pastel colours and line the straight, narrow streets. Right by the sea is the cobblestoned *Avenida Amílcar Cabral*, with some cafés and restaurants, the hospital and a few office buildings. Women offer fruit and vegetables for sale in the shade of the trees and a few idlers pass by; old people sit chatting in the shade. Brightly coloured fishing boats have been pulled up on to the golden sand and the fishermen sit next to them repairing their nets. Further to the south, you will see an 18th century fortress that has been abandoned and left to decay.

FOOD AND DRINK

All of the restaurants are in Vila do Maio.

ESPLANADA WOLF DJARMAI

Chef Wolfgang creates Creole cuisine with a European touch and also produces various varieties of homemade, hot and spicy *malagueta* (piri piri) – be careful when you try it for the first time! Container café with a shady terrace. *Sun–Fri | behind the church | tel. 9 71 03 31 | Budget*

MARIAMA

Feel like a taste of Africa? This small, blue house is the place to go for the inexpensive lunchtime specials such as **INSIDER TIP** the delicious fish and chicken stew. The ● shop next door does braids *(tranças)* and sells African arts and crafts. *Mon–Sat | near Ana Rita restaurant | tel. 9 21 05 40 | Budget*

CHEZ PASTIS

Prettily decorated restaurant where tasty Creole and European dishes are conjured up using fresh produce. Exceptionally good service, quiet atmosphere, fine selection of wine. *Mon–Sat from 7pm | Av. Amílcar Cabral | tel. 9 95 35 65 | Moderate*

TROPICAL

You can enjoy delicious snacks, main dishes and cakes in this open greenhouse on the beach. The fresh fruit cocktails or their happy hour caipirinhas *(6–7pm)* are also highly recommended! Another plus point: an exchange library with English books! *Tue–Sun | on the outskirts of town | tel. 2 55 18 47 | Budget*

SPORTS & ACTIVITIES

Those with plenty of energy can walk for miles along the white sandy beaches and enjoy the views. There are many worthwhile destinations in the interior of the island and the ☆ *Monte Batalha* (294m/ 8648ft) and ☆ *Monte Penoso* (436m/ 1430ft) can be explored by mountain bike *(bike hire: Esplanada Wolf Djarmai | daily 10am–6pm | tel. 9 71 03 31).* Remember to pack a pair of binoculars in your holiday luggage. The wide, flat expanse of sandy desert is the habitat of bar-tailed larks and coursers such as hoopoes. Osprey and falcons circle high above in the sky. Many birds, reptiles and insects also live in the acacia forests in Calheta and Morro but they are relatively shy.

FUNDAÇAO MAIO BIOVERSIDADE ☺

This nature conservation foundation was established in 2010 and is dedicated to the preservation of the nature on Maio. It also aims to create a sustainable livelihood for the people living there and offers information and a series of great excursions ranging, from turtle and bird watching to the history of salt production. *Vila do Maio | tel. 9 95 90 61 | www.maio conservation.org*

SUNFISH SCUBA DIVING ACADEMY

They offer a series of dive courses from refresher training to diving safaris. Guided snorkelling excursions, rental of fishing and snorkelling equipment and island excursions. *Vila do Maio | tel. 9 54 95 62 | www.capeverdediving.com*

KITE & DIVE GUESTHOUSE MAIO

Nadine offers kite surfing courses and equipment rental (kites, surf and body boards); Franziska gives diving course and rents out all you need for diving and snorkelling. Accommodation is in the affiliated guesthouse with two rooms *(Budget)*, a few hundred feet from the sandy beach that is also suitable for children. *Calheta | tel. 9 52 28 19 | www.kite surfing-maio.com*

BEACHES

There are beautiful beaches all around the island. The beaches on the west coast are ideal for swimming – the beach of fine sand stretches for miles from Vila do Maio to past Calheta. The treacherous currents make the beaches in the north of the island unsuitable for swimming. This is also where the sea turtles lay their eggs in summer and you should not go to the beach during this time. There are also heavenly beaches in the east and south but they are more difficult to reach. You have to take drinking water, food and something to protect you from the sun!

PRAIA GONÇALO
(137 F2) *(Ⓜ Q15)*
Secluded beach on the east coast, with fine white sand and dark lava stones. Fragments of sea snails shells show that this is where fishermen dive for them, break them open and sell the inside flesh *(búzio)*. There is a palm grove further inland.

PRAIA DE MORRO
(137 E3) *(Ⓜ P15)*
Magnificent white sandy beach, while its dangerous currents make it unsuitable for swimming it is perfect for taking a walk. However, a large holiday complex disturbs the idyll somewhat.

PRAIA DE PAU SECO
(137 E2) *(Ⓜ P15)*
This rocky beach on the west coast is well suited for snorkelling. It can be reached by walking along the beach from Calheta.

PONTA PRETA
(137 E3) *(Ⓜ P16)*
A high plateau south of Vila do Maio that has unfortunately been defaced by uncontrolled development. A perfect, golden sandy beach with small caves in the colourful rocks stretches for 6km/3.7mi to the east. Not always suitable for swimming. Around 30 minutes walk.

PRAIA DE SANTANA ★
(137 E2) *(Ⓜ P15)*
A somewhat hidden beach – with dunes up 25m/82ft – north-west of Morrinho. Although there are strong winds, it is suitable for swimming. Walkers can find bizarre boulders and desert roses.

ENTERTAINMENT

KABANA BAR
This wooden pavilion at the town beach is right in the midst of the action. It is the ideal place to enjoy a reasonably priced meal and to meet Cape Verde locals and holidaymakers from other countries. *Daily, Sun only to 6pm*

KULOR CAFÉ
Good music, great atmosphere, fabulous homemade *pontches,* wine by the glass. Excellent food, also during the day. *Mon–Sat | Vila do Maio | Rua Cidade de Laures, opposite Supermercado Pick & Pay*

WHERE TO STAY

CASITA VERDE
Friendly guesthouse with two rooms near the beach, five minutes from the centre. Garden with large ☀ shady terrace and sea views. Also INSIDER TIP guided tours of the island and art courses. *Vila do Maio | Fontana | tel. 2 55 20 66 and 9 96 06 33 | www.casita-verde.de/index_en.htm | Budget*

JARDIM DO MAIO
Well-run guesthouse with a view of the harbour and rooms with private bathroom. A fan helps in the heat. Two ☀ rooftop terraces overlook the sea. *3 rooms | Vila do Maio | Av. Amílcar Cabral | tel. 2 55 11 99 | Budget*

PORTO INGLÊS
Modern, well-equipped guesthouse near the health centre. *7 rooms | Vila do Maio | Rua di Povo | tel. 2 55 16 98 | rpingles@cvtelecom.cv | Budget*

APARTMENTS ROSA DO MAIO
Guesthouse with four rooms and three apartments with kitchen and bathroom, near the beach. *Vila do Maio | Fontana | tel. 2 55 11 99 | Budget*

RESIDENCIAL INES
Self-catering option – either in a studio with kitchen unit or in a more spacious apartment with an additional bedroom. Well equipped, with a view of the countryside or the sea. *20 units | Vila do Maio | Fontana | tel. 9 93 70 22 | Moderate*

STELLA MARIS
Six different sized apartments and a detached villa in a closed holiday complex with swimming pool, under Italian management. Well equipped, with terrace and sea view. *Ponta Preta | tel. 9 93 70 22 | Moderate*

TORRE SABINA ☀
Stay in an impossibly romantic white-washed tower! The entrance is downstairs, the living room with balcony on the first floor and the bedroom at the top. Comfortably furnished, bathroom with hot water, a sun terrace, and the beach is right on the doorstep. *Calheta | tel. 2 56 12 99 | http://inseltraum.biz/english/torre-sabina-home/ | Moderate*

The turtles lay their eggs on the beaches of fine sand on Maio's northern coast

SOUTHERN ISLANDS

Yellow, green, pink, turquoise, blue: the pastel coloured houses shine in all shades. The islands' colourful colonial architecture is an eloquent witness to the history of Cape Verde.

And you will encounter this history everywhere on the southern islands of Santiago, Fogo and Brava – in the buildings, in the people's consciousness and in their music. The history of Cape Verde began on the south islands. The first European settlers started living on Santiago in 1461. As a Portuguese colony, the island soon became an established staging post in the growing slave trade. The children of European immigrants and African slaves were the first representatives of the Creole people.

Settlement in Fogo began in 1500 and it was intended that a drastic form of class segregation would preserve the weakening feudalism of the European, which had failed on Santiago. This worked for 250 years. Brava was used as a holiday province from the 18th century – an isolated ivory tower far removed from the murderous heat and raging epidemics.

The three islands have very different landscapes. The volcano island Fogo, with the second highest volcano in the Atlantic, stands out in all respects of the word. It is the hottest of all the Cape Verde Islands.

Photo: São João near Port Gouveia on Santiago

Volcanoes and a colonial past: in search of Cape Verde's natural and human history

Brava and Santiago are medium-height mountainous islands that are suitable for agriculture. The main crops grown on the slopes of the hills are maize, beans, fruit and sugar cane. The increasing drought has hit these islands particularly hard. The history of the archipelago manifests itself most clearly on the southern islands: you will discover the roots of the Creole people on Santiago, the geological crea-

tion of the islands on Fogo and an unspoilt way of life that has changed little over the centuries on Brava.

SANTIAGO

(136 A–C 2–5) (*M–O 14–17*) **Santiago is the main island of Cape Verde and at 383mi² it is also the largest. It has the**

One of the oldest buildings in Cape Verde: the Convento de São Francisco

most inhabitants and is agriculturally, economically and historically the most important.

Nowhere else in Cape Verde are there more houses, more cars, more doctors, more money and more crime. Santiago is the island of superlatives.

The topography is formed by two mighty mountain ranges: the ꗝ *Pico d'Antónia* nature reserve with the highest mountain on the island (1394m/4573ft) and the Sierra Malagueta (1064m/3491ft). In between, there are a series of intensively cultivated high plateaus with steep precipices. More than half of all Cape Verdeans live here – around 270,000 – and two of the three largest cities in Cape Verde are on Santiago. These are the capital city Praia and the dynamic centre of agricultural trade Assomada.

Santiago is the most African of all the islands. Its culture and traditions are characterised by an especially strong African influence because this island always had the closest ties to the continent. Its traditions are more closely linked to African roots and this is particularly noticeable in the music and language. The islanders call themselves *badios* in contrast to the *sampadjudos* – their name for the inhabitants of the other islands. Their fascinating history remains alive in their songs and dances such as the *batuco* and *funaná*.

SIGHTSEEING

ASSOMADA (136 B4) (*ロ M16*)

If you're planning on going, then you must visit Assomada (pop. 12,000) on a Wednesday or Saturday – the market days. The market is the engine and heart of the city, a folksy, popular venue with a brisk trade in everything from pigs and chickens to clothes, baskets, fish and bananas. The Catholic church and town hall are on the main square the *Praça Gustavo Monteiro* with the culture centre on the opposite side. There you will find a small shop that sells traditional arts and crafts, such as *panos* and jewellery. Unfortunately, it is not always open.

CIDADE VELHA ★ (136 B5) *(𝕄 N17)*

This is where settlement of the archipelago began. Immediately after their discovery, the Portuguese claimed the Cape Verde Islands as a colony and the first military base started operating within less than a year. Four years later, the first settlers arrived. To promote the outpost under its former name of Ribeira Grande (today's official name: Ribeira Grande de Santiago), the Portuguese king gave the residents the right to keep slaves in 1466. The Portuguese royal family's idea was to establish a feudal system and use slave labour to develop a flourishing agricultural sector. The plan failed due to the notorious lack of water and harsh climate but this did not mean economic bankruptcy — its favourable location made Cidade Velha (pop. 1200) a major hub in the rapidly growing slave trade between Africa, Europe and America. The pillory

on the village square is a reminder of those days. Some other reminders of the colonisation period that still remain include the *Nossa Senhora do Rosário* church, the ruins of the *Convento de São Francisco* and the *Catholic cathedral* as well as the ☆ *Fortaleza Real de São Filipe* fortification complex high above the village.

PRAIA ★ (136 C5) *(𝕄 N17)*
MAP INSIDE BACK COVER

Cape Verde's capital city is located in the south-east of Santiago. The city, which today has a population of 130,000, succeeded Cidade Velha (15km/9.3mi

> **CITY** **WHERE TO START?**
> Up to the **plateau**! That is the centre of Praia and it is where all of the interesting sights in the capital are: the old colonial houses, town hall and church, the culture centre, the vegetable market and Museu Etnográfico are only a few minutes' walk away from each other.

MARCO POLO HIGHLIGHTS

Women spending a few meditative moments in the Nossa Senhora da Graça church

away) as the seat of government in 1731 because it had one decisive advantage: a 40m/131ft high plateau that was easy to defend against pirates. From that time on, things improved for the city and its population steadily grew. Although other cities have frequently contested Praia's dominant political and economic position over the past 400 years, today it is firmly established as the country's capital. There is particularly fierce competition with Mindelo. The harbour city on São Vicente was able to make a strong economic and cultural position for itself in the 150 years of its existence; Praia's advantages are mainly of a political and commercial nature. Praia has now come to set the tone in lifestyle, art and culture.

The *plateau* still forms the centre of the city, in earlier days it was the residential district, today most of the rooms in the pastel coloured colonial houses are occupied by shops and offices but it remains the most interesting part of town for tourists. Discover the *historical buildings* and the *vegetable market* on the broad main street Avenida Amílcar Cabral, the main square Praça de Albuquerque with the ● *Nossa Senhora da Graça* church (where you should not miss the *10am* Sunday mass), and the *town hall*. This is also the site of the *Palácio da Cultura (Mon–Sat 10am–5pm | Av. Amílcar Cabral 17 | free admission)*, which gives you an impression of Creole culture with its art exhibitions and other cultural events. You can buy delicious baby bananas and sweet papayas from one of the many women selling fruit in the surrounding side streets. The *Museu Etnográfico de Cabo Verde (Mon–Fri 9am–6pm | Rua 5 de Julho 45 | entrance fee 100 CVE)*, founded in 1997, shows its treasures in the pedestrian precinct. Historical articles of everyday life and displays describe the way life used to be on the different islands.

A bustling market for all kinds of goods the ● *sucupira* is held in the *Várzea* district from Monday to Friday. You will find mountains of shoes next to the latest electronic toys from China at the countless stands. Right alongside, bikinis in all the colours of the rainbow flutter in the breeze; at the next stand t-shirts, football jerseys and fabrics with African patterns flap in the wind next to glittery ball dresses ... The upper class *Prainha* district is on a peninsula to the west. Stately diplomat villas and private estates surround well manicured parks and form the perfect backdrop for elegant hotels with panoramic views of the Prainha and Quebra Canela beaches.

RUI VAZ (136 B4) (*Ⓜ N16*)

The village of Rui Vaz (pop. 1000) lies at an altitude of 800m/2625ft in the midst of breathtaking mountain scenery. This is the starting point for visits to the *Pico d'Antónia* nature reserve with Monte Xoxa and all its antennas. A narrow, steep path leads down (400m/1312ft) from the village to *São Jorge dos Orgãos* where Cape Verde's agricultural research institute has been established, which also runs a small ● *botanical garden (Jardim Botánico | no set opening times | free admission)*.

SERRA MALAGUETA ✂ (136 A–B3) (*Ⓜ M15*)

The Serra Malagueta is in the island's north. Until well into the 1980s, when a road was built through the rugged range, the more than 1000m/3280ft high mountains separated Tarrafal from the rest of the island. The Serra Malagueta is now a nature reserve. Its 1913 acres has 26 species of endemic plants as well as endangered reptiles and birds. The most well known endemic bird is the Cape Verde kingfisher. A small ◔ *shop (Tue–Sun | on the road from Assomada to Tarrafal)* in the park administration building sells *panos* and other authentic Cape Verdean arts and crafts. Brochures in English and Portuguese provide information on the nature reserve; there is also a toilet and small snack bar.

TARRAFAL ★ (136 A2) (*Ⓜ M15*)

Tarrafal (pop. 7000) is located in the hot north-west of Santiago. The small semi-circular bay has a beach of white sand fringed with coconut palms that sway gently in the breeze. A dozen colourful fishing boats lie on the edge of the ocean. The fishermen set out in their boats shortly before sunrise and return around midday ● when the market women and the

SANDY VARIATIONS

Pristine white beaches on the eastern islands, magical bays of black sand in the north and south. The black sand is made of weathered volcanic stone of the – geologically speaking – still relatively young islands. At Tarrafal on São Nicolau it contains iodine and titanium and is said to help those suffering from rheumatism if they wrap it in a cloth and lay it on the painful part of the body. The light sand on the east islands is the product of eroded island rocks. This group of islands is considerably older and is made up of fossil sediment rock and coral deposits. Sand brought by the winds from the African continent is added to the local variety. Fine white sand from the Sahara drifts up to 700km/435mi across the Atlantic before being deposited on the east side of the islands.

interested gather at the shore to inspect the catch. As soon as the shopkeepers have carried away their selection in large bowls, peace returns to the coast.

The name Tarrafal brings back painful memories in Portugal as the former concentration camp – where the fascist Salazar regime used to torture and mur-

BAIA VERDE ☆

The hotel restaurant on the rocks above the bungalow complex serves refined traditional and international cuisine. Especially tasty – but not always available: INSIDER TIP the fresh tuna sandwich (sandes de atum). Daily | Tarrafal | Moderate

Colourful fishing boats on the beach in Tarrafal waiting for the next catch

der resistance fighters and critics – is just a few miles away. A tiny museum (no set opening hours | entrance fee 100 CVE) displays pictures and documents (only in Portuguese).

FOOD & DRINK

ALTO MIRA

Tarrafal's French chef makes the best pizza far and wide! The fish dishes are also very good. Friendly atmosphere in a charming courtyard. Daily | Tarrafal | tel. 9 96 38 65 | Budget

FLOR DE LIZ

Local cooking, fresh every day. You can keep your children happy with a pizza and select your own breakfast in the morning from all of the various goodies available. Daily | Praia (Plateau) | Rua 5 de Julho 43a | tel. 2 61 25 98 | Budget

BAR JOSÉ DA ROSA

The veteran of all Cape Verdean snack bars is located in the pedestrian precinct not far away from the vegetable market– it has been operating since 1947! In addition to all kinds of snacks (such as fried moray eel – *moreia frita*), there is a daily special at lunchtime and you can also have breakfast here. *Daily | Praia (Plateau) | Rua 5 de Julho 9a | tel. 2 61 38 93 | Budget*

CAFÉ PÃO QUENTE

Just follow your nose: it will lead you straight to a huge selection of tasty bread and cake specialities from their own bakery. To take away or eat on the spot in the INSIDER TIP café in the gallery. *Daily | Praia (Plateau) | Rua Andrade Corvo 16 | tel. 2 61 47 50 | Budget*

PENEDINHO

This is where the locals eat; the wonderful sea view is the same as in the restaurant next door but the food costs only half the price – and is just as scrumptious. *Daily | Cidade Velha | on the seashore | Budget*

O POETA

One of the most popular restaurants in town, and rightly so – delicious food, fine wines, friendly service and a large roof terrace with sea views. Especially recommendable: fish and seafood. *Daily | Praia | Achada de Santo António | tel. 2 61 38 00 | Budget*

CAFÉ SOFIA

The place to see and be seen! Chic pavement café opposite the university, where foreign diplomats and guests like to stop for a cup of coffee or a drink. *Daily | Praia | Praça Luís de Camões 31a | tel. 2 61 42 05 | Moderate*

SHOPPING

The markets on Santiago are particularly colourful and lively. In *Praia* the vegetable market and the *sucupira*, where all kinds of goods are sold, are open from Monday to Saturday; it is worth visiting *Assomada* on Wednesday or Saturday. Monday and Thursday are the best days for a market spree in *Tarrafal*. That is when you can also buy clothes, shoes, bags, arts and crafts, and much more in the market hall on the road to Assomada.

INSIDER TIP GALERIA BÉYA

This is the place to buy good arts and crafts from Cape Verde and Africa, such as lava objects from the island of Fogo, jewellery, *panos* etc. *Praia (Plateau) | Rua Andrade Corvo 12*

HARMONIA

Well stocked music shop where you can listen to the CDs before you buy. They also sell instruments, guitar strings, postcards, etc. *Praia | Rua Visconde de Sao Januário 19*

LOW BUDGET

▶ It is famous all over Cape Verde: the goat's milk cheese from Fogo. Traditionally, it comes in the form of a mushroom in a narrow ring of green agave leaves. One of the places where it is especially inexpensive is in São Felipe's market hall where an entire cheese only costs 150–200 CVE.

▶ Spend a night in private accommodation *(casa de campo)* when you visit the *caldeira* on Fogo. It is not only the cheapest way but also makes it possible for you to participate in the lives of the people and get some fascinating insights. The tourist office has information on people who rent rooms *(see p. 71)*.

SANTIAGO

SPORTS & ACTIVITIES

DIVECENTER SANTIAGO
It is run by Georg and Monaya, two well known diving experts, and it is hard to imagine a more beautiful spot. Great dive sites in the bay that is part of the King Fisher Resort (only a few minutes by boat). Monaya is a specialist in underwater archaeology and an author. *Tarrafal | tel. 9 93 64 07 and 9 92 30 50 | www.divecenter-santiago.de/start/?language=en*

SOUL TOURS
A wide selection of excursions to Santiago, Sal, Fogo, São Vicente and Santo Antão ranging from visits to dance and music rehearsals to four-day alpine trekking. Andreas (Swiss) and Milton (Swiss/Cape Verdean) will make you acquainted with all of the facets of nature and the people living here. *Tarrafal | tel. 2 66 24 35 and 9 17 85 29*

TUTUTOURS
Bartolomeu de Barros shows you his home country on hikes, city walks and island tours by car. *Praia | tel. 2 62 77 54 and 9 84 67 91 | tututours@yahoo.com*

BEACHES

Santiago used to have magnificent bathing beaches on the east coast. However, the massive removal of sand for construction purposes has changed that. The locals are fond of the beaches in *Calheta de São Miguel* (136 B3) *(ᗢ N15)* and *Pedra Badejo* (136 C3) *(ᗢ N15–16)*. The *Praia Baixo* (136 C4) *(ᗢ O16)* is difficult to reach but especially beautiful. There are some picture-perfect beaches in the north-west. The alarming pollution in the *Praia Gamboa* in Praia below the plateau makes it inadvisable to go into the water there.

INSIDER TIP PRAIA DA PRATA
(136 A3) *(ᗢ M15)*
The 'silver beach' in Ribeira da Prata is a little known gem. It is only a few miles south of Tarrafal and you will often have the whole beach to yourself. A green valley opens up to a wide beach with fine dark sand and coconut palms. Well suited for swimming.

PRAIA DO TARRAFAL
(136 A2) *(ᗢ M15)*
The island's beautiful showpiece beach is located in a sheltered bay in the north-west – and it deserves all the praise it gets. It is a dream of a beach with soft white sand, lined with palm trees where you can still experience life in a genuine fishing village. Wonderful for swimming, relaxing or just watching.

PRAINHA/QUEBRA CANELA
(136 C5) *(ᗢ N17)*
Praia's two bathing beaches are located to the left and right of the *Ponta Temerosa* promontory with its lighthouse. White sand between dark rocks and a couple of acacia tress to provide some shade – a popular beach with families.

ENTERTAINMENT

5AL DA MÚSICA
You simply must go! The restaurant is actually famous for the unforgettable performances given by famous musicians but the chef is also an artist in his own right. Live music every evening; ● *batuco* dancers swing their hips on Tuesdays. *Mon–Sat | Praia (Plateau) | Av. Amílcar Cabral 70 | tel. 2 6 11 6 79*

ZION
Hip and trendy: this is the place to be seen at the weekend. The chic disco is in the modern Palmarejo district and attracts

crowds of fashionably dressed revellers. *Thu–Sun | Praia (Palmarejo)*

WHERE TO STAY

BAIA VERDE

34 bungalows under palm trees only a stone's throw from the sea. Kingfishers flit among the palm fronds and a cheeky monkey may steal a banana out of your hand. This makes it easy to ignore some small technical flaws. *Tarrafal | tel. 2 66 11 28 | www.baiaverdetarrafal.com | Moderate*

HOTEL HOLANDA

Cosy Dutch Cape Verde hotel with a relaxed atmosphere and international guests. Located in a vibrant residential and commercial district five minutes away from the city centre. *10 rooms | Praia | Achada Santo António | tel. 2 62 39 73 | www.hotel holanda.com | Budget*

INSIDER TIP KING FISHER RESORT

Ten wonderful apartments in tasteful, natural stone buildings and five rooms (minimum stay: four nights). Very good facilities, private terrace. Located above a private bay, right near the water. The resort has its own dive base. *Tarrafal | tel. 2 66 11 00 | www.king-fisher.de/index.php?l ang=en | Moderate*

HOTEL PESTANA TRÓPICO

International four star hotel in the upmarket residential district with two salt water swimming pools, near the beach. The hotel's Alex Restaurant *(Expensive)* is considered the best in town. *47 rooms, 4 suites | Praia (Prainha) | tel. 2 61 42 00 | www.pestana.com | Expensive*

PRAIA MARIA

15 charming, clean rooms right in the centre. Good value for money, but rather loud. *Praia (Plateau) | Rua 5 de Julho | tel.*

Palms sway gently in the breeze at the Praia do Tarrafal

2 6143 37 | *res.praiamaria@cvtelecom.cv* | *Moderate*

PRAIAMAR OÁSIS
ATLÂNTICO HOTEL ✹

Good restaurant with a panoramic view (*Expensive*), salt water pool, sauna, and facilities for disabled guests. The hotel's ● *Panorama Bar* with a view of the Atlantic is one of the loveliest spots in Praia for a sundowner. The Sunday brunch includes the use of the pool and attracts many non-resident guests. *Praia (Prainha)* | *tel. 2 6141 53* | *www.oasisatlantico.com* | *Moderate*

INSIDER TIP▸ POUSADA QUINTA
DA MONTANHA ☺

Modern mountain lodge in keeping with ecological standards, at an altitude of 800m/2625ft on the edge of the Pico d'Antónia nature reserve. Perfect hiking area and excellent cuisine with ingredients from the pousada's own organic garden. Lavish Sunday lunch buffet in the garden restaurant (*Moderate*). *28 rooms* | *Rui Vaz* | *tel. 2 68 50 02* | *quintamontanha@cvtelecom.cv* | *Moderate*

INFORMATION

There is an information kiosk at the *Praça Alexandre Albuquerque (Mon–Sat 9am–6pm)*, in *Praia* and a tourist office in *Cidade Velha (Mon–Sat 9am–6pm | Largo do Pelourinho)*.

FOGO

(*139 D–F 2–5*) (*⍟ G–H 16–18*) **The name says it all: the island of Fogo (Portuguese for fire) is an active volcano. Circular, almost 3000m/9840ft high, with a cone measuring 25km/15.5mi at the base and 9km/5.6mi at the top of the caldera.**

The base of the crater is at an altitude of around 1700m/5577ft and is enclosed to the west by a gigantic semicircle of jagged, almost 1000m/3280ft high walls of rock. The perfectly shaped cone of the active volcano – the Pico do Fogo – rises up out of the bizarre black and grey lava ash landscape on the eastern edge. It is 2829m/9281ft high making it the highest mountain in Cape Verde. Enormous rivers of lava – pitch black or grey depending on their age – snake their way down from the caldera to the ocean and hot sulphurous vapours force their way out of gaping vents on the precipitous east flank.

The north-east side of the island benefits from the trade winds that make it fertile and very green. Citrus, mango, banana trees and coffee bushes give the area around Mosteiros on the coast a feeling of the tropics. This is also where you will find the forested Monte Velha area; a dense forest of eucalyptus trees and conifers. There are fertile volcanic ash fields on the northern slopes where the grapes that are used to produce the *vinho de Fogo* grow in shallow hollows.

Agriculture is even carried out in the caldera. Around 700 people live in the Chã das Caldeiras. The total population of the 184mi² island is 37,000. Approximately half of them live in the São Filipe region on the west side and a quarter in the north near Mosteiros. A surfaced ring road around the island connects the isolated farmsteads and villages.

SIGHTSEEING

CHÃ DAS CALDEIRAS ★
(*139 E–F3–4*) (*⍟ H16–17*)
Black slopes covered with scree, high lava rocks and grey ash fields form the bizarre backdrop to the two villages of *Bangaeira* (pop. 300) and *Portela* (pop. 400). There is every imaginable shade of grey – the

soil, roads, houses and walls – all tone on tone. Only a few colourfully painted doors and bright clothes provide a contrast. The buildings of lava, concrete and sandstone are low with sloped roofs to collect rainwater and wine and agricul-

eyes – a fascinating contrast to their coffee-coloured skin. The French nobleman settled on Fogo in 1872, built irrigation channels and roads, improved the medical care and introduced winegrowing to the Caldeira.

The donkey is still the most sensible means of transportation on Fogo

ture are also planned to make use of every drop of water. When the reservoir of the summer rainfall has been used up, new supplies must be brought in by truck – saving water is not just a catchword here! There is only running water in some tourist accommodation while the locals have to collect it in buckets as they have done for so many years.

Quite a few of them have a common ancestor: the French Count Artmand Montrond. Many children have blonde hair and blue

MONTE VELHA ☀ (139 E3) (*Ⅲ H16*)

In the 1940s, acacia, cypress, pine and eucalyptus trees were planted on a large scale on the northern flank of the volcano. Today the forest on Monte Velha is one of the largest wooded areas on Cape Verde. It is always cool and misty here; the delicate yellow and green lichens that cover the trees collect water from the air and transform the forest into a INSIDER TIP surreal wonderland where you can go for wonderful walks.

Get an insight into the everyday life in Cape Verde at the market in São Felipe

MOSTEIROS (139 F2) *(Ⓜ H16)*

Mosteiros (pop. 750) lies in the green, subtropical north-east of the island in a picturesque location between steep mountain slopes and the ocean. A few rather rundown manor houses are remnants of the colonial past. The ☼ church square is right on the waterfront and provides a lovely view of the rocky coast. Coffee, papaya, mango and banana plants flourish on the green slopes above the town. The main growing region for Fogo coffee is in the area around Mosteiros. The Monte Velha cloud forest stretches from the town up to the crater.

PICO DO FOGO ★ ☼
(139 E3) *(Ⓜ H17)*

The Pico do Fogo, or Pico for short, last spewed lava and ash in 1785. The peak crater that the eruption left in its wake is 500m/1640ft wide and 150m/492ft deep. A hike on the Pico takes around four or five hours and you will be rewarded with magnificent views into the caldera and often across the Atlantic as far as Santiago. Hikers will have to deal with a 1100m/3600ft difference in altitude so you need to be in good physical shape and have a sturdy pair of hiking shoes. It is compulsory to be accompanied by a guide; this can be arranged locally in the *tourist office (tel. 2 82 15 39)*, in the wine cooperative shop *(Loja da Cooperativa)* or in the *Pousada Pedra Brabo*. The half an hour descent down the steep ash field (lots of slipping and sliding) is an absolutely unique experience. The ascent begins very early in the morning and it is therefore necessary for you to spend the night before in the Caldeira.

PICO PEQUENO ☼
(139 E3) *(Ⓜ H17)*

The crater that erupted in 1995 is on the western flank of the Pico. You have to climb up a good 200m/656ft before you can look into the caldera that spewed lava the last time it erupted. Yellow sulphur and red iron oxide deposits paint eccentric images on the black basalt, there is the smell of sulphur in the air and if you put some dry grass into one of the cracks in the rocks it will suddenly burst into flame. The spectacular backdrop is formed by two gigantic gas craters.

SÃO FILIPE ★ (139 D4) (*m G17*)

The capital of the island (pop. 8100) is located on a 70m/230ft high plateau on the west coast. It was founded around 1500 as the second settlement on Cape Verde. Portuguese aristocratic families were granted the land from the crown as a fief and established a strict hierarchy. The aristocratic upper class lived in the lower town *(Bila Baixo)* separated by a wall from the slaves who lived in the upper town *(Bila Riba).* The social differences were also reflected in the architecture of the houses, the rich lived in elegant *sobrados* – two storey houses with balconies and airy central courtyards – the most beautiful are now listed monuments. One of them is now a private museum run by Monique Widmer, a Swiss expat. The ● *Casa da Memória (Wed–Fri 10am–noon | free admission | www.casadamemoria. com.cv)* has furniture, household objects and historical photos, as well as a garden with endemic plants. The ● *Museu Municipal de São Filipe (Mon–Fri 8am– 1pm and 2–6pm, Sat 8am–noon | entrance fee 100 CVE)* is just a few houses away. Along with the other exhibits, you will be able to see a typical slave hut *(funco)* in the courtyard.

The *Igreja Nossa Senhora da Conceição* church with its sky-blue façade and *town hall* on the concrete covered Praça 12 de Setembro are both located in the lower town. The *vegetable market* is just around

BOOKS & FILMS

▶ **The Last Will & Testament of Senhor da Silva Araújo** – by Germano Almeida (translated by Sheila Faria Glaser) this tale of Señor da Silva's rise from being a have-not to a prosperous businessman is a humorous portrait of Cape Verdean society. The book was also made into a film (Napomuceno's Will) by Francisco Manso in 1997 starring Nelson Xavier with Cesária Évora in a minor part

▶ **Cape Verde: Crioulo Colony to Independent Nation** – by Richard Lobban is a fascinating study of Cape Verde's history from the slave trade to independence. It explores the country's cultural heritage, economics and politics (Westview Press,1998)

▶ **Transnational Archipelago: Perspectives on Cape Verdean Migration and Diaspora** – edited by Luís Batalha explores subjects such as language and music and the impact of the Cape Verdean diaspora (Amsterdam University Press, 2008)

▶ **The Origin of The Cape Verdean Nationality** – a short video about the history of the islands with a focus on the music and dance traditions that date back to the time of slavery *(www. youtube.com/watch?v=XZgu-gocaaQ)*

the corner. There is plenty of hustle and bustle in the neighbouring streets in the morning. Women sell their fruit and fish on the roadside while loud hammering and sawing can be heard coming from the many carpenters' workshops. American jeeps and motorbikes bump along over the potholed road. They are noisy proof of the close ties between Fogo and the United States that developed through generations of emigration. The unhurried atmosphere of the small town, with its little bright blue cottages, seems like the ideal world of a doll's house.

The *Praia da Fonte Bila* beach with its glittery black sand stretches for miles below the steep coastline. The former fortification complex *Fortim Carlota*, which served as a prison until 2005, dominates the scenery. A paved path leads down to the beach below the fort. Unfortunately, it is no longer safe there – do not go on any strolls on the beach if you are alone! There is no danger of being attacked in the city itself because there are always plenty of people nearby.

FOOD & DRINK

All of the restaurants we recommend are in São Filipe.

CALEROM

Good local fare and an attractive patio make this a popular choice with the locals. Try the tasty grilled dishes or the fish in coconut sauce. *Daily | Rua de Pato | tel. 2 81 32 96 | Budget*

CHURRASQUEIRA AFRICANA

Grilled fish, meat and chicken; inexpensive and delicious. There are often freshly prepared stews such as the ● INSIDER**TIP** *djagacida* a typical Fogo dish. Live music on weekends. *Daily | Rua Jaime Mota | tel. 2 81 32 59 | Budget*

INSIDER**TIP** PIPI'S BAR

African cuisine that is hard to beat. Pipi, a young Senegalese woman, prepares fabulous grilled chicken and her peanut sauce is pure poetry. Great cocktails and live music on Friday evenings. *Daily | next to the Hotel Savana | tel. 9 71 58 83 | www.pipis-bar.com | Budget*

SEAFOOD

Well-established restaurant with many local regulars. The fish and seafood are served at tables on a cliff above the Praia da Fonte Bila. *Daily | opposite Fortim Carlota | tel. 2 81 26 23 | Moderate*

TROPICAL

The courtyard does justice to the name: subtropical flair under shady trees, colourful wall paintings. Traditional and international cuisine, fish specialities. Try the 'Romeo and Juliet' dessert. Cocktails in the evening, live music on Friday and Saturday. *Daily | tel. 2 81 21 61 | Budget–Moderate*

SHOPPING

Loja da Cooperativa ۞
Everything is straight from the producer: the shop run by the wine cooperative INSIDER**TIP** is the most inexpensive place to buy Fogo wine, as well as liqueurs, aperitifs and the potent grappa *(bagaçeira)*, coffee and other local specialities. *Chã das Caldeiras | Portela | tel. 2 82 15 33 and 9 96 54 35*

SPORTS & ACTIVITIES

Climbing and bouldering in a unique environment: Mustafa Eren *(Chã das Caldeiras | Bangaeira | tel. 2 82 16 62 | musti@blocsyndicate.com)* is a trainer for sport climbing and will guide you up or down. The gigantic crater wall around the caldera is the perfect place for two-day climbing treks and you will also be taken into the depths of two eruption caves. Mustafa provides the high-quality equipment and can explain things in detail.

BEACHES

The strong surf and treacherous currents make swimming dangerous on Fogo. Ponta da Salina is the only beach that is safe all year round

PONTA DA SALINA (139 E3) *(₪ G–H16)*

Fogo's best swimming beach is around 15km/9.3mi north-west of São Filipe. A rocky bridge separates a pool from the ocean. There is a small – but unfortunately not particularly clean – sandy beach between grottoes, caves and black basalt reefs. Accessible from the road to São Jorge where a narrow road branches off down to the coast.

PRAIA DA FONTE BILA (139 D4) *(₪ G17)*

The wide, black sandy beach below São Filipe stretches for miles but swimming is dangerous.

ENTERTAINMENT

FOGO LOUNGE ●

Enjoy cocktails and fruit juices sitting in gigantic wicker chairs under the open sky. Also a good place to be during the day – the snacks (pizza, sandwiches, pancakes) are especially recommendable. *Tue–Sun | São Filipe*

The rocky Ponta da Salina bridge separates the swimming pool from the ocean

LUA NEGRA

The place to be at the weekend – great atmosphere, live music, tasty cocktails, cold beer ... there is usually not much action before 9pm but then it soon fills up. The Italian Cape Verdean dishes prepared by the owner Max can also be recommended. *Tue–Sun | São Filipe | Zona Cobom, near the Hotel Xaguate*

BAR RAMIRO

This is the place for music – every evening and in a very special style. Ramiro's father leads the group and sometimes his son David also joins in. The homemade wine *manecon* is just as typical as the music. *Daily | Chã das Caldeiras | Portela*

WHERE TO STAY

CASA BEIRAMAR ⚘

The lovingly restored historic colonial house opposite the church has four rooms and apartments, all with bathroom, terrace and sea view across to Brava. *São Filipe | tel. 2 81 34 85 | Moderate*

POUSADA BELAVISTA

Beautiful manor house in colonial style in the centre of town. The 17 rooms are all individually decorated. The breakfast coffee served here is fabulous. Reservations absolutely essentially, they are often fully booked. *São Filipe | R. Achada Pato | tel. 2 81 17 34 | p_belavista@yahoo.com | Budget*

CHRISTINE E IRMÃOS

Relaxed guesthouse with ten charming rooms on the main street. Good, inexpensive restaurant *(Budget)* with traditional regional cuisine. *Mosteiros | tel. 2 83 10 45 | Budget*

CASA DE LAVA

The five rooms with shared bathroom (hot and cold water) are simple and clean. Cecilio Montrond is one of the best guides if you want to climb the volcano and his wife Elena is a fabulous cook. *Chã das Caldeiras | tel. 9 88 21 27 | Budget*

INSIDER TIP ▶ CASA MARISA

Ten attractive, very clean rooms, most of them with private bathrooms and running water. If you order in advance, Marisa the owner will delight you with her wonderful meals. *Chã das Caldeiras | Bangaeira | tel. 2 82 16 62 | www.fogo-marisa.com | Budget*

OPEN SKY

Modern guesthouse in the upper section of the town. Rooms with air conditioning, TV, refrigerator. The restaurant *(Budget)* is well known for its good traditional cuisine. *10 rooms | São Filipe | tel. 2 81 27 26 | majortelo@yahoo.com | Budget*

SAVANA

The 16 rooms in this two storey historic colonial house are grouped around a small patio with a swimming pool. All of the rooms are air conditioned and have TV. Really peaceful! *São Filipe | tel. 2 81 14 90 | www.hotelsavanafogo.com | Budget*

TCHON DE CAFÉ

Twelve cheerful rooms in the middle of a banana grove. The restaurant *(Budget)* specialises in regional dishes, seafood and *petiscos* (snacks). *Mosteiros | near the church | tel. 2 83 16 10 | gennybarbosa@hotmail.com | Budget*

INSIDER TIP ▶ TORTUGA

Nicely decorated, cosy little guesthouse on the beach far away from the hurly-burly. A place where you can forget everything going on around you! Around 20 minutes walk from town or only a couple of minutes by taxi. If you pre-order, Roberto the proprietor cooks fabulous meals *(Moderate)*. *4 rooms, 1 bungalow | São Filipe | tel. 9 94*

15 12 | www.tortuga-fogo.eu/index.php/bb/?lang=en | Budget

HOTEL XAGUATE

Comfortable four star hotel right on the steep coast. Garden, ✻ swimming pool with sea view. *39 rooms | São Filipe | on the road to the harbour | tel. 2 81 50 00 | www.hotelxaguate.com | Expensive*

from Fogo. The peaks of the almost 1000m/3280ft high mountains are usually hidden under clouds because Brava lies in the lee of Fogo.

This is an advantage that has moulded the character of the island: the cloud cover means that the dew does not evaporate and benefits the island's vegetation which is luxuriant. From October

Even dragon trees flourish on Brava, the green island

Tourism office Chã das Caldeiras | Mon–Sat 9am–1pm and 3–6pm | tel. 2 82 15 39

BRAVA

(138 B–C 4–5) (🗺 F17–18) Circular and hardly 10km/6.2mi in diameter: Brava (pop. 6800) is the smallest of the inhabited islands of Cape Verde.

Brava is located in the south-west of the archipelago about 20km/12.4mi away

to February the island is a green oasis with verdant pastures, man-high maize and flowers blossoming everywhere. In this season, Brava's nickname of the 'flower island' is completely justified: oleander, bougainvillea, jasmine and hibiscus in every shade imaginable flourish in these months. Dragon trees are also indigenous. However, the aridity of the past hundred years has made the springs and summers considerably more barren than in former times; some typical plants such as the urzela lichen are now almost extinct.

The turquoise church in Fajã d'Agua appears to be almost white in the dazzling sunlight

Visitors arrive at the island via the port of Funa on the east coast: a handful of cube shaped houses make their way up the hill behind the tiny bay. A cobblestone street leads steeply upwards, bushy acacia branches hang down over the lanes; prickly agaves cling to rocky ledges. The higher up you go, the cooler the air becomes. The island capital Nova Sintra is at an altitude of 500m/1640ft while the highest point is the mountain massive *Monte Fontainhas* (976m/3202ft) is 3km/1.8mi to the south. The sleepy village of Fajã d'Água lies on the west coast. Things were much livelier in the 19th century when American whaling ships signed on seamen and loaded provisions here. The close relationship of the islanders to the east coast of the United States continues to this day.

From a geological viewpoint, Brava is actually an extension of Fogo: volcanic activity there can be felt as quakes on Brava. Work on the island is scarce as its isolated location is a hindrance to economic progress. So far, there is hardly any infrastructure for tourism and the ship connection to Fogo is also not always reliable. If you plan to visit Brava, you should be flexible and allow two or three days of leeway on both sides of your stay. But once you get here you will discover a hiking paradise.

SIGHTSEEING

FAJÃ D'ÁGUA ★
(138 B4) (*Ⅲ F17*)

This harbour village (pop. 120) is in a rocky bay that was formed by a flooded volcano crater and used to be important for whaling. Bizarre black rocks tower up out of the crystal clear turquoise water. There is only room for a handful of houses in the area between the dark pebble beach and the massive mountain; most of them stand in a row along the shore. Tattered coconut and date palms sway in the wind. There is a turquoise coloured church at the northern entrance to the village. The beach is not suitable for swimming but there are some natural seawater pools in the rocks not far away.

FONTE DE VINAGRE (138 B4) (*⌀ F17*)

The Fonte de Vinagre (vinegar spring) lies in a wide valley below Nova Sintra. The water contains fluoride and bicarbonate and tastes slightly sour. Take a sip! It is said that the water has curative properties and in times gone by the ill used to come here to bathe. There are terracotta heads with their mouths wide open on the four corners of the old 19th century *bathhouse*. A paved path leads down to the spring from Santa Bárbara.

FURNA (138 B4) (*⌀ F17*)

Brava's port village Funa (pop. 600) lies at the mouth of a valley in the north-east of the island. Nestled beneath a concrete rainwater reservoir there are white, blue and grey buildings around the natural bay formed in a crater that was flooded by the sea. The harbour is the only permanent point of access to the island and is protected by towering walls of rock on three sides. A surfaced road winds its way up to Nova Sintra 7km/4.3mi away. The steep 4km/2.5mi long footpath up the mountain is shorter and more attractive.

JOÃO D'NOLE/MATO GRANDE ⚘ (138 B4) (*⌀ F17*)

The two villages of João d'Nole and Mato Grande (pop. 400) are located a little way above Nova Sintra. João d'Nole is a very picturesque little hamlet with well cared for houses and many orchards. The *Igreja Santo Antão,* a small turquoise coloured

church, stands on a rise. Mato Grande is not quite as idyllic as its sister village but makes up for this with spectacular views over the entire eastern coast.

NOSSA SENHORA DO MONTE ⚘ (138 B4) (*⌀ F17*)

The village (pop. 150) is tucked up on a mountain ridge in the north-western section of the central hilly country. The church, which was built in 1826, stands on a large square with a view of the Fajã Valley. The road leading here passes through the village of *Cova Joana* where you will be able to admire some magnificent manor houses.

NOVA SINTRA ★ (138 B4) (*⌀ F17*)

Brava's capital of Nova Sintra (pop. 1500) lies 500m/1640ft above the sea on a fertile plane that is often engulfed in fog. The pleasantly temperate climate led the upper classes and colonial administrators of Fogo and Santiago to build summer residences here in the 18th and 19th centuries. This resulted in the development of a charming little town with streets laid out like a chessboard that was named 'new Sintra' after its Portuguese model Sintra. The main street is lined with what were once elegant manor houses; trees and flowers grow between the wrought-iron lanterns on the median strip. The main streets meet at the park-like *Praça Eugénio Torres*. This is also where you will find the *town hall*, a modern *Nazarene church* and the *music pavilion*. A plaster model shows the relief of the island.

The musician and poet Eugénio Torres (1867–1930) was born in Nova Sintra and was one of the pioneering artists in Cape Verde culture. He composed songs for the simple folk with texts in Kriolu. His baptismal church *Igreja São João Baptista* is located on the eastern outskirts of town. Nearby, a stone replica of *Columbus' ship*

'Santa Maria' awaits St John the Baptist's Day when the townspeople celebrate a festival at the monument.

FOOD & DRINK

O CASTELO

Typical Cape Verde cuisine, always freshly prepared. The *residencial (Moderate)* of the same name provides the best accommodation on Brava so far: six modern, clean rooms with private bathroom. The owner speaks English. *Daily | Nova Sintra | main road to Fajã d'Água | tel. 2 85 10 63 | Budget*

MANUEL BURGO

If you order in the morning, you will be rewarded with delicious local dishes! Accommodation is provided in three simple rooms *(Budget)*. *Daily | Fajã d'Água | tel. 2 85 13 21 | Budget*

SHOPPING

MINI MERCADO POUPANÇA

The best stocked supermarket on Brava – from groceries and drinks to shoes and sanitary supplies. *Nova Sintra | Rua Sossego | tel. 2 85 11 36*

SPORTS & ACTIVITIES

Brava does not have a bathing beach. The only possibility to go for a swim is in the *sea swimming pools* near Fajã d'Água. A stairway south of the village leads down to a handful of rock pools with warm water. If the surf is strong, the waves smash against the rocks – sometimes so violently that it is impossible to swim.

HIKING

Many old donkey trails – some of them paved and most in good condition – criss-cross the highlands. Although Brava is the epitome of a hiking island, hikers are comparatively rare – the island is too remote and difficult to reach. There is no signposting and it is essential that you always have a map of the area with you.

NOSSA SENHORA DO MONTE – FAJÃ D'ÁGUA (138 B4) (*Ⓜ F17*)

A lovely three-hour hike along donkey trails takes you from the mountains down to the Atlantic. The path starts at the *Igreja Nossa Senhora de Monte* and winds its way to Lavadura. There, you go over to the right side of the slope and start your descent to Lagoa. You can either cover the last third by going back along the bottom of the valley or – a bit longer – through the village. The mango trees and coconut palms along the old irrigation channels provide some shade. You then pass through a steep cleft in the valley back to the main path.

NOVA SINTRA – FONTE DE VINAGRE (138 B4) (*Ⓜ F17*)

A pleasant walk that takes about one and a half hours starts at the 'Santa Maria' memorial in Vila Nova Sintra. A steep path directly behind it leads a few hundred feet downhill until it meets the new road. It continues on the other side – always downwards – first of all to Santa Bárbara and finally to the spring. If you find the ascent over the entire stretch too strenuous, you can cover the last section on the road – it is a little longer but not as steep.

ENTERTAINMENT

BAR COQUEIRO

Cool refreshments or hard liquor: this is the place to enjoy *grogue* or the more sophisticated variation: *pontche tropical*. *Daily | Fajã d'Água*

BAR INHO

Small bar with an ample outdoor space where the village youth get together – just follow the lively sound of their voices. *Daily | Nova Sintra | next to Vivi's Place*

WHERE TO STAY

NAZARETH

Well-established family operation with ten rooms, diagonally across from the house where Eugénio Tavares was born. *Nova Sintra | Rua da Cultura | tel. 2 85 11 92 | Budget*

SILVA

Bright, clean rooms with private bathrooms, lounge and kitchen. Relaxed, friendly atmosphere. *3 rooms | Nova Sintra | tel. 2 85 13 49 | tel. 9 96 95 80 | Budget*

SOL NA BAIA

The house is rather nondescript from the outside but it has bright, tastefully decorated rooms with sea views. Sr. José's hobby is painting and he exhibits his works and those of other Cape Verdean artists here. If you pre-order, he serves both lunch and dinner *(Moderate)* and sells homemade *grogue*. *4 rooms | Fajã d'Água | tel. 2 85 20 70 | Moderate*

POUSADA VIVI'S PLACE

Nine rooms, some with private bathroom, grouped around the secluded courtyard of a lovely historic colonial house. Sr. Vivi serves grilled fish and meat in the evening *(Budget)*. This is a popular place for celebrating and it can also be loud next door at night. With internet service. *Daily | Nova Sintra | tel. 2 85 25 62 | pousadavivis-place@hotmail.com | Budget*

There may be no swimming beaches in Fajã d'Agua but the sea pools are just as much fun

NORTHERN ISLANDS

The mighty rocks rise up almost vertically out of the ocean. They have been battered by the wind and weather; deep eroded valleys open up into the Atlantic, jagged gullies split the sand-polished slopes and bottomless ravines yawn between gigantic rocks.

The almost 2000m/6560ft high mountains dominate the appearance of the northern islands. They – and the wind – determine where there will be enough water, where fruit and vegetables can flourish, where people can live. The mountains on São Nicolau and Santo Antão are high enough to stop the clouds blown in by the trade winds, on their north sides there are fertile green valleys where tropical fruit, vegetables and sugar cane grow. There could be no greater contrast to the landscape on the other side of the peaks: nothing but brown desert.

The northern islands were only settled 250 years after those in the south and east. At the end of the 17th century, some Creole families from Santiago and Fogo made their homes on Santo Antão and São Nicolau; European immigrants came from Portugal and Madeira. The population was strongly European right from the very beginning. A Catholic seminary was established in the diocese on São Nicolau in the 19th century and is considered to be the cradle

colonial splendour in pink: the governor's palace in Mindelo

is the capital and lifeblood of the island, he rest is actually not so important. he 88mi² of land is as dry as Cape Verde's desert islands as even the highest peak Monte Verde 774m/254Oft) is not high nough to stop the moisture-laden trade vind clouds. Outside Mindelo, there is not nuch more than brownish–red mountains nd wide, desert-like valleys where hardly nything grows. This is why São Vicente as settled much later than the other ands. Although the sheltered harbour as often used by pirates as a hiding place, e first settlement was only established 1794. The few people who have made eir home in Baia das Gatas, Calhau and io Pedro live an isolated life most of the me. People from town only liven up the lage streets and beach bars when they me here to relax at the weekend. There e small beach bays with white sand from the Sahara on the south-west and east coasts – a fascinating contrast to the dark cliffs.

SIGHTSEEING

CALHAU (131 E4) (ⓜ E4)
The sleepy village of Calhau (pop. 450) is 18km/11mi south-east of Mindelo. It comes alive on weekends when visitors have fun on the beach during the day and then in the bars and restaurants in the evening. The air is full of music, laughter, the roar of motors and loud chatter. On Sunday evening it all returns to normal again.

MINDELO ★ (131 D4) (ⓜ D4)
MAP INSIDE BACK COVER
Mindelo is the second largest city (after Praia) in Cape Verde. The 4km/2.5mi wide bay of a sunken volcano crater pro-

Gigantic mountains and fascinating culture – experience thrilling moments, soulful music and breathtaking panoramas

of Cape Verdean art and literature. The archipelago's most famous style of music has its roots in the port of Mindelo on São Vicente. The town where many popular musicians were born is full of contrasts. The northern islands are a paradise for outdoor holidaymakers and those that leave the beaten track will discover a unique mountain world. Santo Antão and São Nicolau are perfect for individual

tourists and hikers while tracts visitors with the historic metropolis of Mindelo.

São V istoric

SÃO VICEN

inhabitants and almost 70,0

Mindelo – that is Sao V cente

Gigantic mountains and fascinating culture: experience thrilling moments, soulful music and breathtaking panoramas

of Cape Verdean art and literature. The archipelago's most famous style of music has its roots in the port of Mindelo on São Vicente. The town where many popular musicians were born is full of contrasts. The northern islands are a paradise for outdoor holidaymakers and those that leave the beaten track will discover a unique mountain world. Santo Antão and São Nicolau are perfect for individual

tourists and hikers while São Vicente attracts visitors with the historical culture metropolis of Mindelo.

SÃO VICENTE

(130–131 C–E 4–5) *(ᗰ D–E 4–5)* **75,000 inhabitants and almost 70,000 are in Mindelo – that is Sao Vicente. Mindelo**

Colonial splendour in pink: the governor's palace in Mindelo

is the capital and lifeblood of the island, the rest is actually not so important.

The 88mi² of land is as dry as Cape Verde's desert islands as even the highest peak (Monte Verde 774m/2540ft) is not high enough to stop the moisture-laden trade wind clouds. Outside Mindelo, there is not much more than brownish-red mountains and wide, desert-like valleys where hardly anything grows. This is why São Vicente was settled much later than the other islands. Although the sheltered harbour was often used by pirates as a hiding place, the first settlement was only established in 1794. The few people who have made their home in Baia das Gatas, Calhau and São Pedro live an isolated life most of the time. People from town only liven up the village streets and beach bars when they come here to relax at the weekend. There are small beach bays with white sand

from the Sahara on the south-west and east coasts – a fascinating contrast to the dark cliffs.

SIGHTSEEING

CALHAU (131 E4) (*∅ E4*)

The sleepy village of Calhau (pop. 450) is 18km/11mi south-east of Mindelo. It comes alive on weekends when visitors have fun on the beach during the day and then in the bars and restaurants in the evening. The air is full of music, laughter, the roar of motors and loud chatter. On Sunday evening it all returns to normal again.

MINDELO ★ (131 D4) (*∅ D4*)
MAP INSIDE BACK COVER

Mindelo is the second largest city (after Praia) in Cape Verde. The 4km/2.5mi wide bay of a sunken volcano crater protects the rather large – but still picturesque – town. The *Fortim d'el Rei* fortress is enthroned on a ☀ hill above; the *Monte Cara*, a rock that wind and weather have eroded and now resembles a human face, stands guard in the west.

Flashy jeeps and designer sunglasses show that it is possible to make money in this town – and that also applies to the rapidly growing middle class. Well-dressed office workers and small business owners are part of Mindelo's cityscape; they soften the contrast between the wealthy financial wizards and scruffy have-nots. The harbour metropolis attracts all those with hopes – hopes for high profits, a job or even just money for the next *grogue*. Around 150 years ago, British immigrants, Creole slaves and sailors from all over the world flooded into the rapidly growing boom town and created a dynamic, cosmopolitan mixture. Bars and a red-light district sprung up creating a special kind of culture with the unique music styles such as *morna* and *coladeira*. The musical and architectural heritage from that era established Mindelo's reputation as Cape Verde's cultural metropolis today.

Nowhere else on the Cape Verde Islands are there as many colonial buildings. Magnificent government buildings and stuccoed manor houses line the shady squares and the broad *Avenida Amílcar Cabral* road that runs along the shore. There is even a smaller version of Lisbon's Torre de Belém from the 1820s to be admired and next door is the fish market with plenty of hustle and bustle among the stands with their silvery fish, colourful headscarves and t-shirts. Women selling fish, fruit and vegetables, sweets and cigarettes can also be seen across the street. The *Rua Lisboa* starts a few hundred feet towards the harbour. This is the heartbeat of the city with numerous small cafés and shops and already plenty of activity in the in the morning. In the historic market hall you can look down on mountains of fruit and vegetable from the upper gallery with its shops and bars. The *town hall*, *Nossa Senhora da Luz* church (1863) and the classicist pink *governor's palace* are all just

MARCO POLO HIGHLIGHTS

a few steps away. Well-established – and old-fashioned – guesthouses and chic new hotels welcome their guests on the commercial street *Avenida 5 de Julho*. It leads to the *Praça Nova*, the most popular place to take a stroll in Mindelo. In the evening, people get together on the paths in the park around an ornate art nouveau pavilion to see and be seen and ● on Sundays local families promenade in all their finery to the music of a brass band. The contrast between nostalgic colonial flair and the mirror façades of the new buildings is just one of many: in Mindelo there is a strong contrast between the rich and poor; intellectuals and artists live next to beggars and alcoholics, the business mogul with his luxurious yacht rubs shoulders with the shoe shiner. The growing middle class observes all of this with cosmopolitan sangfroid.

MONTE VERDE ☀ (131 D4) *(𝄢 D4)*

On a clear day, one has a magnificent panoramic view of Mindelo's harbour bay from the summit of Monte Verde. It is also often possible to see as far as Santo Antão and the uninhabited islands of *Santa Luzia, Branco* and *Razo*. After leaving Mindelo, travel about 5km/3mi towards Baía das Gatas where there is a turn-off to the *Monte Verde Nature Reserve.* The road leads up to the plateau in a series of wide curves – you can drive, but it is far better to walk.

SÃO PEDRO (130 C5) *(𝄢 D4)*

A handful of small, cube shaped, pastel coloured houses, a bar and a couple of shops: São Pedro (pop. 1000) is a peaceful, languorous fishing village. It is located below two mountain flanks on the southwest coast only a stone's throw away from the airport. Depending on the wind and weather, the white sandy beach offers great conditions for surfing and swimming but sometimes only for going for a walk.

VULCÃO VIANA ☀ (131 E5) *(𝄢 E4)*

The geologically young volcano is only around 3km/1.8mi south of Calhau. It has not been very affected by erosion so far and its volcanic rock structure is very easy to see.

FOOD & DRINK

In many cases, the restaurants and cafés outside of Mindelo are only open on weekends.

003

Tiny, dark and well hidden: Sr. Dani has served lunch since 1998 and every day there is something different and it is always good. You should definitely try the best *pasteis de natas* (puff pastry filled with custard) in Mindelo! The owner speaks English. *Mon–Sat | Mindelo | Rua António Aurelio Gonçalves 3 | tel. 2 31 48 82 | Budget*

ARCHOTE

Often recommended, and rightly so. International cuisine, regional and local dishes. Tue, Fri and Sat, live music. *Daily | Mindelo (Alto São Nicolau) | Rua Irmãs do Amor de Deus | tel. 2 32 39 16 | Moderate*

PASTELARIA BETTENCOURT

This is where the locals come to eat: daily lunch specials and everything is tasty and inexpensive. **INSIDER TIP** Come early; it is always packed after 1pm! *Mon–Sat | Mindelo | Avenida da República 27 | tel. 2 31 28 44 | Budget*

INSIDER TIP ▶ CENTRE CULTUREL FRANÇAIS

The café in the French Cultural Centre is a peaceful oasis. Enjoy the cakes, hearty snacks and daily specials in the shady courtyard. *Closed Sat evening and Sun | Mindelo | Rua de St° António 1 | tel. 2 32 11 49 | Budget*

CHAVE D'OURO
Nostalgic charm with white tablecloths, on the first floor of the guesthouse of the same name. The fish dishes are particularly good. *Daily | Mindelo (Alto São Nicolau) | Av. 5 de Julho | tel. 2 32 70 50 | Budget*

LE FLOSTEL
The best pizza in town; numerous different varieties. Popular with the locals. *Daily | Mindelo (Alto São Nicolau) | tel. 2 31 43 20 | Budget*

GAUDI
Choice of Hungarian goulash, chicken breast in honey and many other dishes that are unusual in Cape Verde, but they also serve local specialities. Live music every evening. The Hotel Gaudi *(10 rooms | Budget–Moderate)* on the upper floor is modern, clean and centrally located. Free Wi-Fi. *Daily | Mindelo | Rua Senador Cruz 5 | tel. 2 31 89 54 | www.hotelgaudimindelo.com | Budget*

CAFÉ LISBOA
Small, dark and traditional – for decades, this has been where Mindelo locals have come to enjoy their morning coffee. *Closed Sat evening and Sun | Mindelo | Rua de Lisboa | Budget*

CASA MINDELO
Meeting place for guests from around the world with a large selection of cakes, sandwiches, main courses and desserts, as well as a soup of the day and lunchtime specials. You will feel like you are in a commune if you stay in one of the four cosy rooms *(Budget–Moderate)* on the upper floor; shared bathroom, kitchen, living room

Thanks to its location (and despite its size) Mindelo is a picturesque town

and terrace. *Mon–Sat | Mindelo | Praça Dom Luís | tel. 2 31 87 31 | www.casacafe mindelo.com | Moderate*

MERCADO MUNICIPAL
Down-to-earth: a chilled, **INSIDER TIP** Cape Verdean Strela draught beer can be had for half of the normal price in the market hall. *Daily | Mindelo | market hall, first floor, stairway to the right, second shop on the right | Budget*

INSIDER TIP SANTO ANDRÉ
The place for gourmets! After his retirement, the Swede Per fulfilled his dream and opened a restaurant in Cape Verde. His team includes his wife and seven other people; the chef is Etienne from Burkina Faso. He serves his select dishes from noon to 3pm and at dinner time. There is grilled suckling pig on Sundays. *Tue–Sun | São Pedro | opposite the Hotel Foya Branca | tel. 2 315100 u. 9 7117 65 | Budget*

SHOPPING

CENTRO CULTURAL DE MINDELO ●
CDs, Cape Verdean handicrafts including **INSIDER TIP** batiks made by the artist Sota Coronel, ceramics, dolls etc. *Mindelo | Av. Amílcar Cabral*

GIFT SHOP
Souvenir shop with a wide selection of textiles, ceramics, paintings and CDs. *Mindelo | Av. 5 de Julho*

HARMONIA
All that Cape Verde has to offer in the field of music, advice is given and you can listen before you buy your CDs with every kind and style of Cape Verdean music imaginable. *Mindelo | Rua Gov. Calheiros, near Praçinha d'Igreja*

SPORTS & ACTIVITIES

Mindelo boasts the only marina (145 berths) in Cape Verde *(www.marina mindelo.com)*. If you don't have your own boat, you can charter a yacht or take part in a sailing trip *(bookings: www.BoatCV. com, www.trend-travel-yachting.com)*. Divers and surfers with their own equipment can indulge in their passions off the coast near São Pedro and kite and windsurfing is also possible on the beach near the fishing village of Salamansa. Ola and Marc from *Kite Surf Now (tel. 9 87 19 54 |*

HOT STONES

The Cape Verdes Islands are the peaks of gigantic submarine volcanic mountains. They formed over 135 million years ago. The three eastern islands settled down about 26 million years ago but those in the west kept on evolving until they reached a height of almost 3000m/ 9850ft. The only volcano that is still active on the islands is on Fogo. When it last erupted in 1995, the people living near it were able to walk to safety before the glowing lava buried the soil, buildings and roads before it. The majestic shield volcano of the Pico do Fogo is also the highest peak in Cape Verde. The most impressive calderas can be seen in Chã das Caldeiras on Fogo (9km/5.6mi diameter), the underwater crater in the harbour at Mindelo (4km/2.5mi) and the Cova do Paúl on Santo Antão (800m).

Praia Grande is popular with sun-worshippers

www.kitesurfnow.eu) offer training courses and can provide the necessary equipment (English speaking).

You can book excursions on São Vicente and to the neighbouring islands at the *Tourist Information Pont' Água (tel. 9 11 03 70)* near the marina or from *Cabo Verde Safari (tel. 2 32 90 44 and 9 91 15 44 | www.caboverdesafari.com).*

BEACHES

There are wonderful beaches all around the island. However, the strong surf and dangerous currents mean that only a few are suitable for swimming. And on all of them you must take your own sunshade!

BAÍA DAS GATAS (131 D4) (*Ø E4*)

The most popular bathing beach on the island – and the most famous in Cape Verde – lies 12km/7.5mi east of Mindelo. Every year in August, tens of thousands of

people make a pilgrimage to the Festival Baía das Gatas that is renowned for its good musicians and infectious atmosphere. Protected by volcanic rocks that reach down to the sea, the semicircular bay forms a wide sheltered lagoon. The sea is shallow until far out from the beach; swimmers dive into the cool water from a long stone breakwater.

PRAIA DE LAGINHA (131 D4) (*Ø D4*)

Sometimes Mindelo's city beach can be really crowded. Follow the road along the shore to the harbour and then it is straight ahead. Also suitable for children.

PRAIA DO NORTE/PRAIA GRANDE (131 D–E4) (*Ø E4*)

These two beaches are south of the Baía das Gatas in a bay that stretches as far as the Calhau promontory. Perfect for sunbathing and walks along the beach; the currents make swimming risky.

SÃO VICENTE

A part of any holiday on Cape Verde: a *noite caboverdeana*

PRAIA DO SÃO PEDRO
(130 C5) *(Ɯ D4)*

Long beach with fine white sand. The strong wind that blows most of the time produces high waves that are a surfer's delight. Swimming is only possible on the west side if the sea is calm.

ENTERTAINMENT

Nightlife in Mindelo means live music! Solo artists or bands play at the ● *noites caboverdeanas* held in almost all restaurants on specific days to accompany dinner. You can find out about who is playing and where from the hotels, tourist information office and flyers. There are also regular concerts in the *Centro Cultural de Mindelo (Av. Amílcar Cabral | Alfândega Velha | tel. 2 31 52 90)* and the *French Culture Centre (Rua de St° António | tel. 2 32 11 49)* – look for the posters. The party continues in the discos – but only at the weekend! They

are empty before midnight and only get really crowded between 2 and 3am.

INSIDER TIP ▶ ALTA LUA

Elegant open-air hotel bar with frequent performances by well known musicians. *Daily | Mindel Hotel | Rua 5 de Julho*

MAY O'LEARY'S

Irish pub with huge leather sofas. Cape Verdean draught beer. *Daily | Rua Cristiano Sena Barcelos (opposite the post office)*

CLUBE NÁUTICO

Billowing jibs form sunshades … food, drinks, interesting people and the latest Cape Verdean news, live music several times a week. *Daily | Av. Amílcar Cabral (Alfândega Velha)*

PAVILHÃO

Mindelo really lets its hair down late in the evening at the weekend in the area around

casionally mixed with Cape Verdean music. *Fri/Sat | Rua Camões, near the Praça Nova*

ARLA
Each of the 13 rooms in the modern, green building above the harbour has its own name. *Mindelo (Alto São Nicolau) | tel. 2 32 86 88 | www.arlaresidencial.com | Budget*

BELEZA
Small, neat hotel, clean and comfortable, with an internet café on the ground floor. 21 rooms with air conditioning, minibar, telephone. Very quiet and only 5 minutes walk from the centre. *Mindelo | Rua Oficinas Navais | Budget*

INSIDER TIP CASA COLONIAL
Beautifully renovated colonial house with different sized rooms and a small swimming pool. Individual guests and small groups will feel at home here; also ideal for families. *7 rooms | Mindelo | Rua 24 de Setembro | tel. 9 11 96 11 | www.casa colonial.info | Moderate*

RESORT HOTEL FOYA BRANCA
10km/6.2mi from Mindelo: holiday complex with six bungalows, twelve suites and 56 rooms in a 7.5 acre garden, right on the beach. Three swimming pools, tennis court, restaurant. INSIDER TIP Lavish Sunday lunch buffet and use of the swimming pool, also for non-guests. *São Pedro | tel. 3 20 74 00 | www.foyabranca. com | Expensive*

JENNY
Panoramic views over the harbour and Monte Cara. 20 rooms with bathroom, TV, refrigerator, air conditioning. *Mindelo (Alto São Nicolau) | tel. 2 32 89 69 | hstaubyn@ cvtelecom.cv | Moderate*

the historic pavilion on the Praça Nova – this is where everybody meets before going on to paint the town red in the pubs, bars and nightclubs in the vicinity. Donna Joya serves her guests cold drinks while they sit and people watch. Try a ● *grogue novo* or INSIDER TIP *pontche de tambarine* (tamarind liqueur)! *Daily | Praça Nova*

BAR PONT' ÁGUA ●
A cocktail or glass of local draught beer tastes twice as good reclining in the shade next to the pool with a view of the marina. You can have a sandwich, crêpe or cake brought to you from the brasserie next door and those who want can take a dip in the pool *(400 CVE). Daily | Pont d' Água | Av. da República*

SIRIUS
Large dance palace with several floors. Mainly young guests who do not show up before 2am. House and techno, oc-

INSIDER TIP **MANUEL BRITO**

The four rooms in Sr. Manuel's private residence. They share two bathrooms and a small kitchen. Wonderful breakfast! *Mindelo | Rua Dr. Medeiros 41b | tel. 2 31 18 51 and 9 92 65 78 | Budget*

MARAVILHA ☆

Twelve spacious en-suite rooms and one suite in a stately villa above the Porto Grande. Good service. *Mindelo (Alto São Nicolau) | tel. 2 32 00 94 | gabs@cvtele com.cv | Moderate*

OÁSIS ATLÂNTICO PORTO GRANDE HOTEL

Renowned four star establishment; the best address in town. Swimming pool, restaurant, and shady terrace, disco. ● Traditional Balinese and foot reflexology massages; also for non-guests by appointment. *48 rooms, 2 suites | Mindelo | Praça Amílcar Cabral | tel. 2 32 31 90 | www. oasisatlantico.com | Expensive*

SOLAR WINDELO

The perfect solution for all needs: three suites, two studios with kitchenette, and two bedrooms; all with bathroom, safe and fan. Nice breakfast terrace and very friendly service. *Mindelo (Alto Santo António) | tel. 2 31 00 70 | www.windelo. com | Budget*

INFORMATION

Tourist information kiosk in *Mindelo (Mon–Fri 9am–1pm and 3–6.30pm, Sat 9am–2pm | opposite the harbour)*. Also guide books, hiking maps, phone cards, postcards and stamps.

All you need to know about São Vicente and the neighbouring islands, as well as excursions and tours, car hire, accommodation, books and postcards and handicrafts in the *Tourist Information Pont d'Água*

(Daily 9am–6.30pm, Sun to noon | tel. 9 11 03 70 and 9 11 00 16 | www.cabocontact. com).

SANTO ANTÃO

(130–131 A–D 1–4) (*∅ B–D 2–4*) **Santo Antão's lifeblood is the road. And that is no surprise with these mountains! They soar vertically skywards with rugged, eroded valleys and dizzying precipices to the left and the right.**

Constructing a road in this terrain is a real adventure. The surfaced road across the island was built 40 years ago and the route along the eastern coast completed at the end of 2008. The ☆ most beautiful of all the routes in Cape Verde leads from Porto Novo, where you arrive on the island, 1400m/4593ft uphill and back down again diagonally across the island to its capital Ribeira Grande. That is the starting point of the road – a remarkable feat of engineering that runs along the coast to Ponta do Sol (5km/3mi) in the north-west and to Vila das Pombas (10km/6mi) in the southeast. The extension from Porto Novo was under construction for many years. It makes it much quicker to reach the fertile north-eastern region of the island where most of its inhabitants live.

Sugar cane cultivation is the main source of income. The sugar presses and distilleries in the landscape show what is made from the slender, high canes: the famous *grogue* of Santa Antão – it is said to be the archipelago's best. *Grogue* is just as important as the road and the export of sugar cane liquor as vital today as it ever was. Individual tourism is becoming increasingly important; especially for those who are keen hikers and Santo Antão is ideal for this activity. The 1979m/6493ft high *Tope de Coroa* is, after the Pico do Fogo, the second highest mountain of Cape Verde and the island itself is a unique, colossal mountain scene. Old, paved mule tracks wind their way all over the 300mi² island. The 1170m/3839ft high Cova do Paúl in the north-east highlands has an impressive crater with a diameter of 800m/2625ft. The tropical Ribeira do Paúl valley runs down from this peak to the ocean.

SIGHTSEEING

COVA DO PAÚL ★ ☼
(130 C2) (*∅ D2*)

In clear weather, you will have a fantastic view to the north-east over the entire length of the Ribeira do Paúl all the way down to the Atlantic from the rim of the crater. To the south-west the crater opens up below you. The panorama is especially impressive when the clouds swirl over the jagged edge into the crater.

PONTA DO SOL ★ (130 C1) (*∅ D2*)

Ponta do Sol (pop. 2100) is located on a flat promontory in the extreme north – the northernmost point in the entire archipelago. Two roads lead down from the main square to the small harbour that is somewhat protected by a makeshift breakwater. Since the foundation of Porto Novo, it has only been used by fishermen. The renovated yellow *town hall* (1882), the former *infirmary* with a massive flight of steps leading up to it, and the Catholic *church* with its free-standing bell tower on the left side, are all in the centre of town around a spacious square. Ponta do Sol is a pleasantly quiet little town where holidaymakers can still find everything they need. It is currently developing into the main tourist destination on the island.

Thatched roofed stone houses are typical of the northern islands

PORTO NOVO (130 C3) (*D3*)

The harbour city Porto Novo (pop. 9500) is located in the south-eastern section of the island. This is also where the ferries from Mindelo arrive. They make the trip Ribeira da Torre. The town (pop. 2500) is a bustling meeting place for locals and tourists alike with its wide selection of shops, restaurants and guesthouses. The *Avenida de 5 de Julho* leads into town and

A stroll through Ribeira Grande takes you to squares such as this one

daily and turn what is otherwise a peaceful town into a bustling trading place. The harbour has been expanded and modernised in recent years and it now possible for cruise ships to stop here. A road leads from the harbour to the centre of town where colourful fishing boats lie in the shade of a few acacias on the small beach with black sand. In spite of its importance as a port and as the largest settlement on Santo Antão, Porto Novo's tourist appeal is only gradually increasing; most visitors head off for the other side of the island as soon as they arrive.

RIBEIRA GRANDE ★ (130 C1) (*D2*)

The island's capital lies in the estuary of the two valleys of Ribeira Grande and shows pastel coloured merchant houses in various stages of renovation – or decay. The heart of the town is the main square *Praça Nossa Senhora do Rosário* with the Catholic church. The narrow side streets with their uneven cobblestones lead to a labyrinth of narrow winding lanes with small shops and workshops. Friday evening is the lively highlight of the week – then, everybody in town seems to be out and about.

RIBEIRA DO PAÚL ★ ≋
(130 C1–2) (*D2*)

The greenest place in Cape Verde: huge mango and breadfruit trees, every inch of the ground covered with vegetables or sugar cane with coconut palms, papaya and banana trees in between. The valley winds its way (6km/3.7mi) from the Cova crater down to the Atlantic – a difference in altitude of about 1000m/3280ft! There is so much to see: from cloud forests full of lichens, to banana and coffee plantations, palm groves and fields of sugar cane swaying in the breeze and the abundant water splashing through the streams, reservoirs and canals throughout the year. The village *Passagem* is almost in the middle where an old, decaying swimming pool is hidden in a shady oasis under blue jacaranda and pink bougainvillea bushes.

TARRAFAL DE MONTE TRIGO
(130 A3) (*ſ\] B3)

On the west side of Santo Antão is the wide bay (10km/6.2mi) of Tarrafal de Monte Trigo (pop. 850). If you want to visit this lush, green paradise, you will have to put up with a three-hour journey over an adventurous track. Once there, you will be rewarded for your efforts with the ideal bathing conditions at the black lava sand beach. The sea is usually calm because the high mountains protect the bay from the wind. A place to relax and enjoy nature.

VILA DAS POMBAS
(131 D1) (*ſ\] D2)

Vila das Pombas (pop. 1300) is on the north-east coast around 10km/6.2mi away from Ribeira Grande. It is the main town in the Paúl district and is located at the end of the Ribeira do Paúl where the delta meets the Atlantic. Steep rocks reach all the way down to the bay with its small pebbly beach where the large black rocks are noisily bounced around by the surging surf. The treacherous current makes swimming dangerous here. Coconut palms rustle in the breeze behind the single row of colourful houses. The public buildings – the *church* built in 1885, the *town hall* and

infirmary – are all in the eastern section of the town. A statue of Santo António, the local patron saint, watches over the town from a hill above.

FOOD & DRINK

A BEIRA MAR ⋙

Donna Fátima serves excellent daily specials at an unbeatable price. Her *residencial (Budget)* with ten en-suite rooms, a terrace and lovely view of the harbour is also recommended. *Daily | Ponta do Sol | Rua Central | tel. 2 25 10 08 | Budget*

CANTINHO DE AMIZADE

This restaurant has enjoyed a fine reputation for years and so have its prices. Enjoy fish and seafood, salads, omelettes and spaghetti in the snack bar, the restaurant

LOW BUDGET

▶ It is a good idea to stop one of the many women walking through the streets with plastic boxes balanced on their heads to see all the goods they have to sell. They often have *pasteis* or *rissois* (small, fried pies, 5–15 CVE each) and sometimes delicious, homemade cakes at very inexpensive prices.

▶ The food itself is good and not very expensive but that is topped by the Portuguese white wine that is served by the glass. The *Chave d'Ouro* restaurant in Mindelo (*daily | Av. 5 de Julho | Rua Lisboa, first floor*) is also a cheap place to spend the night. But be warned: the rooms on the top floor have had some break-ins!

or on the INSIDER TIP lovely, shady patio. *Daily | Ribeira Grande | Rua Padre Fernando Barreto | tel. 2 211 3 92 | Budget*

TROPICAL

Traditional restaurant with a wide selection of fish and meat dishes and excellent wines. The hotel-like guesthouse *(12 rooms | Moderate)* offers good service. *Daily | Ribeira Grande | Hirondina Maria da Graça Rocha | tel. 2 211 1 29 | residencial tropical@hotmail.com | Moderate*

O VELEIRO

Freshly caught fish served above the roaring Atlantic. Regional cuisine, excellent coffee. Often live music on the weekend. *Daily | Ponta do Sol | at the harbour | Moderate*

INSIDER TIP VONY

Small but really impressive! Everything here is fresh from the sea and absolutely delicious. Also many regional liqueur specialities. *Daily | Ponta do Sol | tel. 2 25 15 39 | Moderate*

SHOPPING

EKI EKO

Arts and crafts and jewellery made by various artists, Cape Verde music, regional specialities, a large selection of postcards (with stamps) and hiking maps. Marie France makes INSIDER TIP lamps and other accessories from banana leaf and jewellery from natural material, as well as all kinds of other pretty souvenirs to take home with you. *Ponta do Sol*

CHEZ SANDRO

There are arts and crafts, coffee that is grown nearby and many kinds of homemade liqueurs made with local *grogue,* at the top of the Ribeira do Paúl. You will be able to enjoy a cup of freshly brewed Santo Antão coffee on the small terrace with a view over the countryside. There are five rooms and a dormitory (shared bathroom) if you decide to stay for the night. *Daily | Cabo da Ribeira | tel. 2 23 19 41 | sandro_lacerenza@yahoo.fr*

SPORTS & ACTIVITIES

CABO VERDE BIKES

Mountain bike rental and organised tours. A pick up in Porto Novo can also be arranged. *Ponta do Sol | tel. 9 82 50 59*

MANGALA

A variety of fishing boat trips, snorkelling or excursions (such as rock barnacle harvesting), hikes to local destinations and to Tope de Coroa, as well as night-time expeditions to see turtles laying their eggs, etc. *Tarrafal de Monte Trigo | tel. 2 27 60 71 | mangala-tours@hotmail.com*

BEACHES

Santo Antão's coast is rugged with steep cliffs, rocks and reefs and it is equally rough under water. Strong currents and heavy surf make swimming dangerous; there are only two good bathing beaches.

PRAIA DE ESCORALET (124 C3) *(ळ D3)*

There are three small bays with black sand beaches approx. 25 minutes' walk from Porto Novo. Very popular with families on weekends because children can swim safely.

PRAIA DE TARRAFAL
(124 A3) *(ळ B3–4)*

The long crescent-shaped sand and pebble beach below the village of Tarrafal de Monte Trigo is a real beauty. A few trees provide some shade. In the eastern section of the bay the rocks stretch down to the sea and bizarre grottoes and caves have been hollowed out. They continue under the surface of the water and form a fine area for snorkelling and diving with plenty of marine life.

HIKING

There is a wide range of hiking routes at all levels of difficulty on the island. Deep gorges, tropical valleys, the steep coast, forests and volcanic landscapes allow for demanding ascents, as well as leisurely strolls. You can make most of the hikes on the well preserved donkey paths without a guide; these include the easy hikes through the Ribeira do Paúl or from Cruzinha to Ponta do Sol where orientation is not difficult. However, only experienced hikers should tackle the more complicated routes. A guide is absolutely essential in the isolated, western plateau! INSIDER TIP Contact Jean Jacques Neves *(Ponta do Sol | tel. 9 99 54 52 | residencial psol@cvtelecom.cv)* who speaks, English, French and Portuguese or the Swiss expat Hans Roskamp *(Ponta do Sol | tel. 2 25 12 13)*.

CRUZINHA – PONTA DO SOL
(130 B–C3) *(∅ C–D2)*

One of the most impressive hikes on Santo Antão takes around five hours and leads uphill and down again for 12km/7.5mi along the coast with a difference in altitude of a good 500m/1640ft. However, you will be rewarded for your efforts with the play of light and colour and the gigantic rock formations. After you leave Cruzinha, continue in a westerly direction and follow the path past the football pitch and

Santo Antão's coastline is wild and rugged

SANTO ANTÃO

The colourful houses in Fontainhas are clustered on a promontory

bizarre eroded rocks that lead to the steep zigzag descent to the abandoned village of Aranhas. Thereafter, the cliff path leads to the small village of Forminguinhas and then on to Corvo, where you can buy cold drinks and use the toilet in the *Pontinha de Giada (tel. 2 25 11 68)*. You then continue hiking to the hamlet of Fontainhas – high up on a rock ledge – before reaching your destination, Ponta do Sol.

ESPONGEIRO – ÁGUA DAS
CALDEIRAS ⬩⬩⬩ (130 C2) (*Ⓜ D2–3*)
Enjoy the fabulous panoramic views of Santo Antão's magnificent mountains on this looped hike on the eastern plateau. In clear weather you will see São Vicente and possibly even as far as São Nicolau. Your trek takes you over dusty trails and donkey paths through the small village of Morro de Vento and the Água das Caldeiras valley to the Casa Florestal, the forester's house.

ENTERTAINMENT

BEIRA MAR
Popular nightclub that attracts many visitors from the surrounding areas. Only open on weekends – not all of them. *Fri/Sat | Vila das Pombas*

POR DO SOL ARTE
Very pleasant both indoors and outside. And there is usually somebody there looking for a chat or wanting to start a music session. The evening meal can also be recommended. *Daily | Ponta do Sol | beach promenade*

WHERE TO STAY

CASA DAS ILHAS
This pretty establishment with nine rooms – five are en-suite, the others share two showers and three toilets (all with hot water) – for one to six people is located

in the centre of the lush, tropical, Paúl valley. Ten minutes' walk and you can arrange to have your luggage collected. *Ribeira do Paúl | tel. 2 23 18 32 | casada silhas@yahoo.fr | Moderate*

CECÍLIO 🌿

Cecílio and his wife Dirce welcome guests to their house in a picturesque location facing the azure ocean; six bright, clean en-suite rooms with sea views, and delicious breakfasts. Private transfer to and from Porto Novo. *Ponta do Sol | tel. 2 25 14 75 | Budget*

ALDEIA JEROME

Colourful, modern cottage in pleasant surroundings with terrace, playground and rooftop terrace. *6 rooms, 1 suite | Vila das Pombas | tel. 2 23 21 73 | www.aldeia jerome.it.gg | Moderate*

ALDEIA MANGA ☺

Five ecological houses constructed of adobe and natural stone in an idyllic mountain landscape, there is a rather steep walk up from where the car drops you off. Set in more than an acre of garden with fruit trees and a swimming pond. Internet, half-board on request. *Vila das Pombas | tel. 2 23 18 80 | www.aldeia-manga.com | Moderate*

INSIDER TIP ▶ MAR TRANQUILIDADE

Simple comfort in enchanting surroundings: Susi and Frank have created a small paradise of thatched roof stone cottages with shady terraces right on the ocean. A cathedral-like annex completes the ensemble and offers plenty of space – but, it is often fully booked so it is essential to make reservations in advance! Lavish evening buffet with Cape Verdean European cuisine. *Tarrafal de Monte Trigo | tel. 2 27 60 12 | www.martranquilidade. com | Budget*

MARINA DE TARRAFAL

The Spaniard Tomás' small bungalow with private terrace is in the heart of the village but away from all the hustle and bustle. If you pre-ordered, the chef cooks for his guests and takes care of all their wishes. Fabulous breakfast. *3 rooms | Tarrafal de Monte Trigo | tel. 2 27 60 78 | www.marina detarrafal.com | Budget*

POR DO SOL

16 comfortable, air-conditioned rooms with private bathroom in a new building; with restaurant and rooftop terrace. *Porto Novo | Fundo do Lombo Branco | tel. 2 22 21 79 | pordosolpn@cvtelecom.cv | Budget*

SANTANTÃO ART RESORT

70 rooms and three suites in a new four star hotel with swimming pool and tennis court. Black lava beach on the doorstep, various hiking and leisure activities. *Porto Novo | tel. 2 22 26 75 | www.santantao-art-resort.com | Moderate*

SONAFISH

Simple seafront guesthouse in the isolated fishing village of Cruzinha. Two rooms have a private bathroom. Downstairs is a restaurant and bar, they also offer a transfer service. *10 rooms | Cruzinha | tel. 2 26 10 27 | Budget*

TOP D' COROA

This establishment with ten rooms and two suites – all with en-suite, air-conditioning and TV – is new, clean and modern. *Ribeira Grande | Rua d'Água | tel. 2 21 27 94 | www.residencial-topcoroa.com | Budget*

INFORMATION

Information kiosk in *Porto Novo (Mon–Fri 10am–5pm | above the harbour)*.

SÃO NICOLAU

(132–133 C–F 3–5) (𝄞 H–K 5–7) Many regard São Nicolau as Santo Antão's smaller, unprepossessing sister.

The island is not as big, the mountains not as high, the valleys not as deep, the coastline not as steep. But 134mi² island does at least have a unique shape: the west has the same outline as the African continent while the eastern section is a long, narrow promontory. São Nicolau is still an insiders' tip and tourism is not as developed as it is on its larger sister island. There are only two larger towns – the capital of Ribeira Brava in the north-east and Tarrafal, the harbour town, in the south-west. That is where half of the island's 13,000 inhabitants live. The long, narrow eastern section is sparsely populated.

São Nicolau's spectacular mountains make it especially interesting for hikers and explorers and has beaches stretching for miles in the south-west. This is a combination unmatched by any of the islands. The landscape in the south-west is dominated by dry, scorched land. The clouds remain on the north-eastern side of Monte Gordo (1312m/4304ft) and the surrounding mountain slopes where the foothills are green and fertile. Sugar cane, vegetables and tropical fruit grow there on the fertile lava soil of Fajã de São Nicolau.

SIGHTSEEING

CARBERINHO ★ ⋇
(132 C3) (𝄞 H6)

One of the most beautiful places in the archipelago: the bizarre eroded rocks and the raging surf create a spectacular sight. From Tarrafal drive towards Praia Branca until you see a water tank on the right and then, a few hundred feet further on the left, a signpost. Follow the tyre tracks and park your car on the top of the hill – you then hike down to the cliffs. The best way to do this trip is in a hired car with a driver.

JUNCALINHO (133 E3) (𝄞 J6)

The pretty village of Juncalinho (pop. 400) is located on the northern side of the east headland. The small settlement with its traditional little houses is located in a picturesque position on a rocky coast. The *Capela da Sagrada Família* was constructed using natural stone in 1960. Only a few minutes' walk from the village to the north-east, you will find some pools in the rocks that are ideal for swimming.

PRAIA BRANCA
(132 C3) (𝄞 H6)

Ruby red, bottle green, aquamarine blue: the bright colours of the small houses in Praia Branca shine from afar. The pretty,

colourful village (pop. 500) nestles in the valley with steep, winding lanes uphill and crooked steps and paths that lead to hidden corners and idyllic courtyards. From Tarrafal head along the coast to the north-west.

PREGUIÇA
(133 D4) *(Ø J6)*

The tranquil fishing village of Preguiça (pop. 600) on the east coast offers a magnificent view of the eastern semicircle of the bay. It is around 8km/5mi from Ribeira Brava. A road leads down to the Atlantic and you will catch glimpses of yellow and blue, tiled-roof houses high above the sea. You will see the harbour breakwater, the village church and colourful boats on the black pebble beach. At the end of the quay are the ruins of the customs house that was built in 1890. The ruins of a fort – there are still some canons to be seen – and a monument to the

discoverer of Brazil Pedro Alvares Cabral who dropped anchor here in the year 1500, are reminders of the historical importance of the village.

RIBEIRA BRAVA ★
(133 D3) *(Ø H6)*

In 1693, the threat of pirates caused the residents the coastal settlement of Porto da Lapa to leave their homes and establish Ribeira Brava further inland. Today's capital (pop. 2000) lies at an altitude of 200m/656ft in a wide valley with a mighty riverbed. The colonial architecture is still present in the well-preserved trading houses and the *Nossa Senhora do Rosário* cathedral. In 1866, a seminary was established in this diocesan town, it attracted the archipelago's greatest thinkers for years until the Portuguese government closed it in 1917. The unused building on Rua Seminário, on the south side of the river, was donated by Dr. Júlio José Dias

São Nicolau is the only Cape Verdean island with mountains and miles of sandy beaches

(1805–73); his bust has pride of place on the main square the *Praça do Terreiro*. The small park is surrounded by the cathedral, the historic schoolhouse (today, the public library) and some two storey colonial houses. There are many shops and work-shops in the adjacent street as well as a handful of restaurants and guesthouses. An alley opposite the church leads to a small area of greenery in front of the post office and from there visitors are only a few steps away from a park with plane and jacaranda trees next to the deeply eroded riverbed.

TARRAFAL (132 C4) (*◫ H6*)

The seaside Tarrafal (pop. 3700) is the hottest place on São Nicolau. Everything revolves around the port. Fishing boats and cutters bring their catch to the shore and it is then processed in the cold stores and a fish factory. Sometimes, cargo ships unload their freight here. The ferry from Praia to Mindelo – and sometimes even a cruise ship – stops over.

You will discover some charming build-ings if you take a stroll through the centre of the town that is laid out in a grid pat-tern. Old men sit debating on the seaside promenade while children and teenagers swim at the black sand beach.

FOOD & DRINK

CAFÉ ALTERNATIVA

Snacks and main dishes are served in a shady courtyard. Ask for the INSIDER TIP dish of the day. Live music on weekends. *Mon–Sat | Ribeira Brava | tel. 2 35 23 17 | Budget*

The harbour of Tarrafal: a hub for fishing boats, cutters and cruise ships

CASA AQUARIO

If you want to dine at night, you will have to pre-order in the morning. It is worth the effort: Henny Kusters and his team of young chefs conjure up INSIDERTIP fantastic three-course dinners that are unequalled in Cape Verde. *Tarrafal | on the outskirts of town, opposite the hospital | tel. 2 36 10 99 | Moderate*

BELA SOMBRE DALILA

Donna Netinha is a specialist in preparing local dishes *(catchupa, modje, xerém)* and traditional sweets. *Daily | Ribeira Brava | take the street on the right off the main square past the church | tel. 2 35 12 98 | Budget*

FELICIDADE

Tucked away in the northern part of town but easy to find if you ask the way. Some regulars have been coming here for 20 years. Many local fish and meat dishes. *Mon–Sat | Tarrafal | tel. 2 36 11 58 | Budget*

INSIDERTIP CAFÉ DA LAPA

Only those in the know will find their way here: up the hill towards Tarrafal and then left at the colourful mural. Straight ahead and then to the right past the lyceum and keep your eyes open for the sign on the wall on the right after the next intersection. Great traditional dishes at unbeatable prices. Let them know that you're coming two hours in advance! *Mon–Sat | Ribeira Brava | Chãzinha | tel. 2 35 11 36 | Budget*

HOME RESTAURANT MARIA DO CEU

If they pre-order, Donna Maria also cooks local and international dishes for guests who are not staying with her. She rents out a cosy room *(Budget)* with bathroom and ☀ a rooftop terrace with a spectacular view of the coast and harbour. *Preguiça | tel. 2 35 15 82 | Budget*

It's the same everywhere; the locals always know the best restaurant

BEACHES

There are lovely bathing beaches on the west coast of the island as well as in the bay in the south-east *(Carriçal, Preguiça)*. There is hardly any shade at any of them and also practically no infrastructure for tourists.

PRAIA DE BARRIL
(132 C4) (⌀ H6)

This broad sandy beach lies just before the westernmost tip of the island, near a handful of little houses – the hamlet Barril. There is also a solar powered lighthouse. Ideal for swimming, relaxing or going for a stroll.

PRAIA DE CARRIÇAL
(132 D4) (⌀ K6)

The island's most beautiful beach with black sand, acacia trees and coconut palms is located far away on the south-east coast. It can either be reached via a dirt track from Juncalinho or by fishing boat from Preguiça (ask at the harbour).

PRAIA FRANCÊS
(132 C4) *(Ø H6)*

From Tarrafal, take the road to the north until a signpost directs you to the left: the Praia Francês is between the Praia da Luz and Praia de Barril and is a stretch of the coast with fine sand that is perfectly suited for bathing.

PRAIA DA LUZ
(132 C4) *(Ø H6)*

Praia da Luz, with its miles of sandy beach, is located on the west coast north of Tarrafal. Lovely for swimming. However,

the holiday complex that is currently going up is considerably less lovely.

HIKING

São Nicolau offers many interesting mountain and coastal hikes. You can buy hiking maps in the *Pensão Jardim* in Ribeira Brava and book hiking excursions with a local guide from *Blaise Menuet (tel. 9 93 99 20)*.

MONTE GORDO ⋇ **(132 C3)** *(Ø H6)*

You reach the Monte Gordo nature reserve by way of Cachaço. A paved path leads up 600m/1969ft, where you hike through a sparse, mis-shrouded woodland with endemic flora and huge dragon trees. The ascent takes around 3 hours *(see p. 105)*.

Football, a chat, people watching: evening mood in Tarrafal

RIBEIRA FUNDA
(133 D3) (*ɯ H5*)

An easy hike taking about two hours leads from the Estância Bras to the abandoned hamlet of Ribeira Funda. Take a shared taxi on the road from Ribeira Brava to Tarrafal until you reach one of the two turn-offs to Estância Bras. From there a paved path leads along the majestically precipitous coast to *Ribeira de Camarões* where everything is lush and green thanks to the year-round water supply. The small houses in Ribeira Funda come into sight after you cross the last mountain ridge.

RIBEIRA DA PRATA ★ ⛷
(132 C3) (*ɯ H–6*)

On no account should you miss out on the 'pirates' gorge! A donkey track starting in Ribeira da Prata leads up the steep canyon into the fascinating mountain scenery. The little mountain village of Fragata clings to one of the slopes. Even novice hikers will only need about one and a half hours to reach the top – if they have sturdy shoes!

ENTERTAINMENT

GOLFINHO
Cape Verdean dance music and the occasional bit of techno – the local youth party in this trendy venue from midnight until the crack of dawn on Friday and Saturday. *Fri/Sat | Tarrafal | in the centre*

WHERE TO STAY

ALICE
15 rooms, most of them with en-suite, some with air conditioning, others with ceiling fans. The eponymous restaurant *(daily | Budget)*, where Donna Alice serves local dishes, is on the ground floor. *Tarrafal | on the coast road | tel. 2 36 11 86 | Budget*

HOTEL BELA SOMBRA
New, clean and right in the centre: 20 modern, en-suite rooms, air conditioning and TV, internet and laundry service. Sr. Santos also organises island excursions. *Ribeira Brava | tel. 2 35 18 30 | www.bela sombra.net | Budget*

JARDIM ⛷
Guesthouse with eight rooms on the mountain slope. Internet access. Good restaurant *(Budget)* with spacious rooftop terrace and panoramic views. *Ribeira Brava | Chãzinha | tel. 2 35 11 17 | pensao residencialjardim@hotmail.com | Budget*

CASA RAMOS ⛷
Can accommodate up to four people in a two-room apartment with sea views and enormous terrace. *Preguiça | tel. 2 35 15 91 | Budget*

SANTO ANTÓNIO
Modern and clean accommodation. En-suite rooms, air conditioning, centrally located. The restaurant *(Budget–Moderate)* serves hearty Cape Verde cuisine. The speciality of the house is *cabrito* (kid). *13 rooms | Ribeira Brava | Praça do Terreiro | tel. 2 35 22 00 | pensaosantoantonio@ hotmail.com | Budget*

CASA TARTARUGA/CASA PARDAL ☺
Beautiful and secluded location on a promontory over the ocean: two well-equipped holiday cottages – with garden, shady terraces, swimming jetty, stone oven, barbecue, solar energy – invite holidaymakers to relax in complete peace. The guests are also given tips for activities and the information about São Nicolau comes from a real expert: the owner Michael Mary is also the author of the travel guide 'São Nicolau Individual'. *Carriçal | Ponta da Cruz | tel. 2 35 12 13 | www.saonicolau.de/uk | Moderate*

TRIPS & TOURS

The tours are marked in green in the road atlas, the pull-out map and on the back cover

① SANTIAGO: JOURNEY BACK 500 YEARS

The history of Cape Verde is only 550 years old. Cidade Velha on Santiago was the first European settlement on African soil and was declared a Unesco World Heritage Site in 2009. A half-day excursion to the roots of the nation's Creole history and historic buildings will take you to a bygone era.

Cidade Velha → p. 57 is 15km/9.3mi to the west of Praia → p. 57. The taxi or *aluguer* (departures from the Terra Branca roundabout) takes you up hill and down

dale through a dry coastal landscape. The Fortaleza Real de São Filipe fort dominates the scenery 100m/328ft above the town. Get off at the signposted junction and walk the last short stretch on foot. The fort was built in 1587 after the English pirate Francis Drake had plundered the town. With a little imagination, you can visualise how the canons (they are still there) were fired in an attempt to drive the pirate ships away from the coast! When you have had enough of the beautiful views, make your way down into the town. On your way down you will pass the ruins of the Catholic cathedral. It was under construction from 1556 to around

Photo: Cidade Velha on Santiago

Set out on a journey of discovery: you cannot go very far into the hinterland in Cape Verde but you can go quite a way up!

1700; however it was devastated in an assault by the French pirate Jacques Cassart in 1712. Today, the sight of the bright limestone remnants of the apse, the columns on their pedestals and the door frames between the towering remains of the dilapidated walls will send pleasant shivers down your spine.

The pelourinho can still be seen in the centre of the town. Starting in 1512, this is where slaves were sold and criminals punished. At the time, this was not only the centre of the village but also the hub of the intercontinental slave trade. Time for a break? In Casa Velha you can dine with a view of the historic site. The tiny slate cottage has only five tables in the shady courtyard, and one in front of the house, and serves inexpensive local dishes (daily | Largo do Pelourinho | Budget).

A dusty path along the wall on the bank of the riverbed leads into the valley. The Rua Banana, the oldest street in the archipelago, begins on the left. It is lined with tiny cottages in the typical Portuguese building style of the Middle Ages: the house is divided by a corridor with a single room on the left and right. At the end of the street, a few steps lead up to the Nossa Senhora do Rosário church. Construction started in 1495 making it the oldest Catholic church outside of Europe. Stone tombstones inside the church show the last resting place of clerical and aristocratic dignitaries from the 15th to 18th centuries. When the Portuguese navigator Vasco da Gama dropped anchor here on his way to India in 1497, there was not much of the church to be seen; but Sir Francis Drake, the noble English pirate in the service of the queen, visited it in 1585. You will come across the partially rebuilt ruins of the Convento de São Francisco monastery, which was founded by the Franciscans in 1640, if you take the second turn-off to the left from the sandy track. It was destroyed, together with the cathedral, in 1712. You have now earned a cool drink in the shade of the tall mango trees in the Pousada Nacional de São Pedro (daily | tel. 2 67 31 20 | Budget) just outside of town. If you would like to stay here a little longer: the six historic little slate cottages have been renovated and now house an idyllic guesthouse with courtyard (6 rooms | Moderate).

2 FOGO: CAPE VERDE'S HIGH POINT

You will feel like you are on a completely different planet in the bizarre volcanic landscape of the Chã das Caldeiras. The route from São Filipe to the caldera is only 26km/16mi but, up there, it is like being in another universe. You can explore this alien world on foot – the more athletic even climb up to the highest point in the archipelago: Pico do Fogo. But then you should plan on staying overnight.

A series of gentle curves takes you gradually upwards from Fogo's capital city São Filipe → p. 67 through gently rolling hills. The slopes of the mountains, where a few acacias and thorny bushes manage to grow, are cut through by gaping cracks of erosion. You cover the route to Chã das Caldeiras → p. 64 in an ● aluguer. The vehicles depart from the vegetable market in São Filipe at around 11am from Monday to Saturday. First you drive up through hilly terrain with sharp bends and then you will see the first lava flows: wide, dark streams from afar; man-sized stones up close. Then a magnificent panorama – across the wide expanse of hills down to the sea – opens up before your eyes. Black scree and chunks of cinder dominate the scene, while brown soil and plant life become rarer. Then, after one last bend you suddenly catch your first glimpse of the Pico do Fogo → p. 66. The greyish-black, perfectly shaped cone in the middle of this dark lunar landscape is a breathtaking sight! A wooden signpost welcomes you to the Fogo nature reserve as do a few youngsters with souvenirs they have made themselves out of lava stone.

At the foot of the gigantic mountain, fields of coarse, porous rubble make their way through finer layers of ash; rugged ridges and hills of cinder rise up three feet and more. The road cuts a thin swathe through the mighty wall of rock. The black and red crater of the Pico Pequeno opens up to the right of the road and then you reach the village of Portela that stretches along both sides of the road. Medium-height walls made of black lava scree and the box-like houses of grey concrete sandstone almost merge into the surroundings. Only a few blue door frames, the colourful clothes of the people and the bright green vines in the sheltered shallow hollows standout against the monotone background. This is where the Chã wine, with (4km/2.5mi) to the entrance to the Monte Velha → p. 65 nature reserve begins. The hike to the last crater to erupt, the Pico Pequeno → p. 66, takes around 3 hours; the strenuous, demanding climb to the Pico do Fogo approximately 6–7 hours. It is mandatory that you are accompanied

A lunar landscape stretches out from the caldera wall

its unique, fruity aroma, grows – you simply have to try it! In the Tourist Office you can find out more about the Caldeira and its inhabitants and also see a three-dimensional model of how the caldera was formed (Mon–Sat 9am–1pm and 3–6pm | tel. 2 82 15 39).

The neighbouring village of Bangaeira is only 150m away. That is where the trail by a guide! You can spend the night in inexpensive private accommodation, such as the Casa Leopoldo (8 rooms | Chã das Caldeiras | Portela | tel. 9 86 42 93 | Budget) with simple, but clean, rooms with a shared bathroom without running water (bucket water is used for washing and to flush the toilet). If you prefer more comfort, the INSIDER TIP Pousada Pedra Brabo is the place for you *(12 rooms | Portela | tel. 2 82 15 21 | www.pedrabrabo.net | Budget)*. The French chef prepares fabulous food – at prices that are just as fabulous – in the Pousada's restaurant *(daily | Budget)*. The pretty courtyard with a view of the rock face makes the perfect setting.

3 SANTO ANTÃO: PANORAMIC VIEWS

Take a taxi or *aluguer* (approx. 2000 CVE) and travel from Ribeira Grande or Porto Novo up to the Cova crater at an altitude of 1200m/3937ft. From there, you go down 6km/3.7mi to the green tropical valley Ribeira do Paúl and on to the dazzling blue Atlantic. The four to five hour descent presents some breathtaking panoramas; it is steep but not all too difficult.

Before you start the descent, you should enjoy the magnificent views. To the southwest, you have the majestic volcanic crater Cova do Paúl → p. 87 at your feet – a circular area divided into square fields, which are either green or brown depending on the season, with a few small trees scattered about and tiny houses between towering cypresses. Mist often drifts over the crater rim – a spectacular sight! To the north-east, the fertile tropical Ribeira do Paúl → p. 88 valley zigzags its way down to the ocean. Although you are actually above the clouds, you can usually make out the gigantic rugged rock cliffs and the lush terraced mountain slopes

A break to study the map before going down into the Ribeira do Paúl

through gaps in the cloud cover.

A well-trodden paved donkey path winds its way steeply downhill. You wander through a damp cloud forest with the fragrant scent of cypresses, eucalyptus and acacia trees, whose branches are densely covered with fine lichens. Orange, red, violet and yellow flowers sparkle between the bushes. The path leads through fields of scree with impressive boulders and a few trees; lush green ferns line drystone walls coated with white and green lichens. Terraced field of sugar cane and coffee plantations start below the treeline; huge banana trees, yams and rustling papyrus plants are in indication that there is plenty of water here.

You come across the first houses at around 700m/2797ft and the paved road begins a little later. Further down hill, you will find the 🕐 O Curral bar *(daily | Chã de João Vaz | tel. 2 23 12 13 | www.grogue.de/english/index.html | Budget)*. The Austrian owner Alfred Mandl and his wife Christine offer their guests freshly-baked bread, organic salad from their own garden, various types of cheese and other homemade products, which you can also buy. They can also give you interesting information on the people and country – and they have the purest INSIDER TIP *grogue* of the entire archipelago. It is also distilled to Tyrolean standards on the premises and there are several varieties.

From here the steep road leads 5km/3mi further downhill. Shrubs and green bananas hang over the low walls; enormous mango, papaya and breadfruit trees bear a fine harvest of fruit. Coconut palms whisper in the gentle breeze, brooks and streams bubble quietly between the rocks – the Garden of Eden must be just around the corner! You hike past the oasis of Passagem with its violet and pink blossoming flowers on the right hand side and see little thatched roofed cottages

tucked away on the slopes and then – a little further on – one of the rare dragon trees close to the road. You walk through the Eito hamlet and down to the sea and Vila das Pombas → p. 89. There it is easy to find an *aluguer* to take you to Ribeira Grande and then on to Ponta do Sol or Porto Novo.

4 SÃO NICOLAU : DRAGON TREES AND A CLOUD FOREST

You will experience magnificent views on your hike in the mountainous regions of Monte Gordo, the highest peak on São Nicolau. You can either make a leisurely stroll or opt for a demanding hike with steep ascents.

The starting point is in the village of Cachaço (710m/2329ft), that you can reach by *aluguer* from Tarrafal → p. 96 or Ribeira Brava → p. 95. You turn off the main road at the lodge of the Parque Natural Monte Gordo → p. 98 and follow, what is at first, a gentle ascent. You will see some rare dragon trees with their extensive branches, as well as a few isolated farmhouses on the left and right. You soon reach the first trees. Those who decide to undertake the steep climb to the ☀ peak (1312m/4304ft) must be sure-footed and fit. The path through the cloud forest with its lichens takes around three hours and in clear weather hikers are rewarded with a view of a few, if not all, of the islands in the archipelago. If you choose the less strenuous hike, you can turn back whenever you feel like it and pay a visit to the ☀ Nossa Senhora de Monte chapel on the outskirts of Cachaço. There is only one place where the view over the mountains and valleys is more spectacular: at the ☀ viewpoint that is marked with a concrete cross next to the main road half a kilometre away in the direction of Tarrafal.

SPORTS & ACTIVITIES

Cape Verde offers active tourists many sport and leisure opportunities – the desert islands are a paradise for water sports enthusiasts while the mountainous islands are ideal for hikers.

Fantastic sandy beaches – in black or white sand, you can take your pick – invite tourists to relax and take it easy. Bear in mind that there is not much shade and the wild surf and strong currents often make swimming dangerous and there is still not the standard infrastructure for tourists with shops, restaurants and cafés everywhere. There can be some drawbacks if you want purely a beach holiday but this will be made up for by the nature:

a rich bird life, as well as turtles, whales and dolphins, insects and many different kinds of plants make a deep impression on most visitors.

CLIMBING

On Fogo, you can go climbing and bouldering in the breathtaking volcanic landscape of Chã with Mustafa Eren, a qualified guide. He will take you up the 1000m 3280ft high crater wall or down to the volcano's caves. Quality equipment is also provided. *Mustafa Eren | Chã das Caldeiras | tel. 2 82 16 62 | musti@bloc syndicate.com*

Photo: Coral reef

High up, low down, and close to the wind: the island's mountains, dive sites and great surf attract active holidaymakers

DIVING

There are more than two dozen dive sites around Sal but it will always take you at least ten minutes to get to them if you want to see rays, moray eels, surgeon and turtles. The *Orca Dive Club (Santa Maria | tel. 2 42 13 02 | www.orca-diveclub-cabo verde.com)* organises diving courses and trips. The dive sites around Boavista also offer great variety but they are not in the immediate vicinity. Strong swells and stirred sand sometimes limit visibility. Nothing like that happens in the surfer's paradise of Tarrafal on Santiago. There is a 10–40m/33–130ft deep dive area with visibility of over 20m right on the doorstep. *(Divecenter Santiago | Tarrafal | in the King Fisher Resort | tel. 9 93 64 07 | www.dive center-santiago.de/start/?language=en)*.

EXCURSIONS

Whether it's just an excursion or your whole holiday: there are several local English speaking agencies to organise your stay in Cape Verde. *Capverde Escape* organise cultural or adventure custom trips *(www.capverdescape.com)* while *Cabo Verde No Limits* on Santo Antão can satisfy all individual wishes with customised hikes, water sports and island hopping excursions *(Ponta do Sol | tel. 2 25 10 31 | www.cabo verdenolimits.com/en)*.

Hiking, trekking, project visits and cultural activities in the area of music, art and cooking on all the islands are made possible by the services offered by *Vista Verde Tours (São Filipe | Fogo | tel. 9 93 07 88 | www.vista-verde.com)*.

HIKING

Five of the Cape Verde islands have ideal hiking conditions: Santiago, Brava, Santo Antão, São Nicolau and Fogo. The fascinating mountain world is barren and dry from April to August but is beautifully green after the autumn rainfall.

You can climb peaks of up to 2800m/9186ft on ancient donkey paths and explore both rocky deserts and tropical valleys. The hiking maps and guides by Lucette Fortes and Pitt Reitmeyer *(www.bela-vista.net/cape-verde.htm)* are especially recommendable.

SAILING

Water and air temperature never below 20°C/68°F, always a decent sailing wind and crystal clear water with whales and turtles and flying fish that land on your deck just in time for dinner. Pristine beaches and demanding nautical challenges make a sailor's happiness complete. Winds of up to force 8 on the Beaufort scale are not uncommon from November to April; they are not quite as strong in summer.

The sailing experts André Megroz and Kai Brossmann *(tel. 2 32 67 72 and 9 91 58 78 | www.BoatCV.com)* are the authors of a nautical guide to the islands. They offer yacht charters and also make it possible to take part in sailing trips on various routes. *Trend Travel Yachting (email office @trend-travel-yachting.com)* offers similar services. You can book sailing trips with a skipper lasting one or several days on the INSIDER TIP two-master *'Iceni Queen' (tel. 9 95 03 53)*. The trips between and to all the islands in the archipelago are customised to individual needs; up to six people can take part.

SNORKELLING

The strong surf and unpredictable currents mean that snorkelling is only possible in sheltered areas off the coast of the mountainous islands such as in the bays of Tarrafal/Santiago and Tarrafal de Monte Trigo/Santo Antão. The conditions are better on the eastern islands but vision is often limited as a result of stirred sand.

SURFING

Wind and kite surfing is a lot of fun on Sal: the steady north-east trade winds, calm water near the shore, small wind waves and the open swell of the Atlantic with fabulous areas for speed surfing further out. The strong shore break makes it difficult to get started – this means that Sal is not really suitable for beginners. They will find conditions better off the coast of Boavista; the water in the bay of Sal Rei is shallow and there are neither shore breaks nor high waves.

The American multiple world champion Josh Angulo *(Angulo Cabo Verde Windsurf Center | Santa Maria | near Hotel Riu | tel.*

2 42 15 80 | www.angulocaboverde.com)
runs a surf base on Sal. This is the starting
point to set out for areas with different
conditions and levels of difficulty. The *Surf
Zone School (Praia de Santa Maria | Hotel
Morabeza | tel. 9 97 88 04 | www.surf-
caboverde.com)* is located in a relatively
sheltered spot in the bay and also has a
branch on the more difficult west coast.
On Boavista, you can take lessons on how
to manage the board from the Vietnamese
professional surfer François Guy De
Boavista in his *Boa Vista Windclub (Praia
de Estoril | tel. 2 51 10 36 | www.boavista
windclub.com)*. Those who are looking for
a real challenge on the high seas will be
well taken care of on the [INSIDER TIP]
'Itoma' (www.itoma.at/index_en.html):
three surfers designed and built a 23m/
75ft long motor catamaran so that they
(and their guests) can indulge in their
passion for surfing off the Cape Verde
coast.

TURTLE VIEWING

Cape Verde is the third largest breeding
ground for the endangered *Caretta caretta*
turtle. Experience the fascinating reptiles
close up and, at the same time, contribute
to their protection. A nocturnal excursion
to the beach between July and October
will give you the chance to watch them lay
their eggs and bury them in the sand. The
international *Turtle Foundation (Sal Rei |
tel. 2 51 14 38)* runs an observation camp
on Boavista and takes interested persons
on beach controls with their rangers. *SOS
Tartarugas (Santa Maria | near Hotel Riu |
tel. 9 74 50 19 | www.sostartarugas.org)*
does all it can to protect turtles on Sal, as
does the *Fundaçao Maio Biodiversidade
(Vila do Maio | tel. 9 95 90 61 | www.maio
conservation.org)* on Maio. You can also
view the turtles on Santo Antão *(Mangala |
Tarrafal de Monte Trigo | tel. 2 27 60 71 |
mangala-tours@hotmail.com)*.

Surfers don't have to wait very long on Cape Verde's beaches for the perfect wave

TRAVEL WITH KIDS

Cape Verde is a country that is especially fond of children. However, a holiday on the islands with very small children is not really such a good idea – there are some hurdles to overcome. Sunburn and diarrhoea are the two most common complaints. Sun creams with an extremely high protection factor and a hat should definitely be included in your luggage. Holidaying with small children is easiest on Sal and Boavista as some of the larger hotels on those islands have child-friendly facilities but it is most likely that you will have to keep your children amused yourself. Sporting activities or just exploring a foreign environment should keep them happy – children find new things exciting.

EASTERN ISLANDS

MOUNTAIN BIKING
(134 B5) (*Ω R6*)
Children will also enjoy mountain biking on Sal because the island is nice and flat. They can explore the southern part from Santa Maria. It is important to take sun protection and water! Mountain bikes –

also for children – can be hired from *Bebe Beach Rent (Sal | Santa Maria | in front of Hotel Morabeza | tel. 9 70 13 03).*

NEPTUNUS
(134 B5) (*Ω R6*)
The bright yellow craft has an underwater glass observation cabin and is ideal for children to see the tropical submarine world with fish, marine life and sunken wrecks. *Adults 3850 CVE, children 1950 CVE | Sal | Praia de Santa Maria | tel. 9 88 71 07*

SOS TARTARUGAS ☺
(134 B5) (*Ω R6*)
Children can learn all about turtles on educational walks on Sal where they can watch the animals laying their eggs. Every evening from July–Sept. From June–Dec **INSIDER TIP** the rangers provide information on the work they do. Early risers can sometimes see nests being moved. Special activities for children are organised on the beach (changing locations) from July–Dec. *Participation 2200 CVE, children under 10, free | Sal | Santa Maria | near Hotel Riu | tel. 9 74 50 20 | www.sostartarugas.org*

Even without children's clubs, Cape Verde is still a paradise for children with a thirst for knowledge and energy to burn

SOUTHERN ISLANDS

DELTA CULTURA (136 A2) (*M15*)
Learn something new and exciting on holiday at this education centre for children and adolescents. Children can also take part in the football school, learn how to dance the *batuco* or, if they are there at the right time, how to paint and work the lathe. A small contribution is always welcome. *Santiago | Tarrafal | tel. 2 66 27 01 | www.deltacultura.org/en*

DIVECENTER SANTIAGO
(136 A2) (*M15*)
The younger generation is also fascinated by the world beneath the surface of the water. Children over the age of 14 are taught how to deal properly with scuba tanks and flippers. *Junior Open Water Course 420 CVE | Santiago | Tarrafal | tel. 9 93 64 07 | www.divecenter-santiago.de*

NORTHERN ISLANDS

MONTE GORDO NATURE RESERVE
(133 D3) (*H6*)
Children love an adventure and there is plenty waiting to be discovered on a walk through the forest on São Nicolau, a nature reserve full of unique animals and plants. *São Nicolau | Cachaço | www.areasprote gidas.cv/montegordo*

BUFFET AND BATHING
(130 C5) (*D4*)
The four star Foya Branca hotel on São Vicente welcomes non-guests to a lavish Sunday lunch buffet including ● use of the outdoor facilities with three swimming pools – one of them is reserved for children. *Entrance including buffet 1800 CVE, children 900 CVE | Resort Hotel Foya Branca | São Vicente | São Pedro | tel. 2 30 74 00 | www. foyabranca.com*

FESTIVALS & EVENTS

The Cape Verdeans love to enjoy them-selves. Festive town and island celebra-tions on the name day of the local patron saint are common on all the islands. These are the perfect combination of religious and secular traditions: a mass service fol-lowed by a procession through the streets followed by a boisterous festival with an opulent feast, dancing and music. Religious holidays such as Christmas, Easter or New Year are also celebrated extensively and exuberantly with the family and many friends. It is not unusual for several fam-ilies to organise joint weddings, christen-ings and first communion celebrations – the more the merrier!

PUBLIC HOLIDAYS

1 January New Year's Day; **20 January** National Heroes' Day; **March/April** Good Friday; **1 May** Labour Day; **24 June** São João; **5 July** Independence Day; **15 August** Assumption Day; **12 September** National Day; **1 November** All Saints' Day; **25 December** Christmas.
Carnival season starts immediately before Lent.

FESTIVALS & EVENTS

FEBRUARY

Carnival and Creole culture: that means infectious music and seductive samba dancers dressed in feathery costumes – joie de vivre that is contagious. The Cape Verde carnival may be small but it easily compares with the events in Brazil and the Caribbean. The ▶ INSIDER TIP *Mardi Gras in Mindelo* is the most spectacular of all and the ▶ INSIDER TIP *carnival in Ribeira Brava* (São Nicolau) is a fabulous party.

APRIL

▶ *Festa da Bandeira:* the spectacle of the year on Fogo. Hundreds of visitors arrive to celebrate and participate in the seven-day festival in the last week in April with magnificently colourful religious and secular ceremonies. São Filipe is a com-pletely different place during this period. The procession and ▶ INSIDER TIP *tradi-tional equestrian games* are particularly colourful and interesting. The mass in the church and blessing of the flag should not be missed. Just as interesting is the tradi-

Samba and equestrian games: whether a religious festival or just a family occasion, there is always a good reason for a celebration

tional maize crushing: the women pound the maize in a large mortar accompanied by noisy drumming and singing. The festivities reach their climax on 1 May.

MAY

The highlight of the Praia is the ▶ ● *Praia de Gamboa Music Festival* on 19 May. Music groups perform over three nights. Cape Verde's most famous musicians make guest appearances along with stars from Brazil, the Caribbean and Africa.

24 JUNE

The ▶ INSIDER TIP ▶ *Festa São João Baptista* is celebrated on many of the islands. A ritual dance, the *colá de São João,* is performed during the procession that makes its way – to the beat of drums and plenty of yelling and screaming – through the towns and villages. It is led by a person dressed like an admiral (with a colourful

boat around his neck) and his helmsman. They stop every couple of steps to urge the bystanders to dance while women, in twos or fours, follow them dancing to the accelerating rhythm of the drum.

AUGUST

Tens of thousands of spectators flock to the ▶ ● *Baía das Gatas* music festival held on São Vicente in the first weekend in August after a full moon. The wonderful beach is a unique setting for the festival where Cape Verdean, African, European and South American musicians ensure high spirits. Dozens of small stalls offer snacks and drinks. The atmosphere is unbelievable. But beware: pickpockets!

SEPTEMBER

Every year in September the live music at the ▶ *Sal Music Festival* turns the beach into a weekend long party.

LINKS, BLOGS, APPS & MORE

LINKS

▶ www.capeverde.com All about your destination at a glance: categories such as holiday and travel, hotels and accommodation, culture, language, music and much more. Also with videos and live webcams

▶ www.capeverdeweb.com General information (notably about Sal, Santiago, Boa Vista and São Vicente islands) as well as sections on history, culture, climate and a forum where you can ask travel questions

▶ virtualcapeverde.net The virtual portal of the embassy of Cape Verde in Washington DC. National political and economic news and lots of useful information related to Cape Verde

BLOGS & FORUMS

▶ http://groups.yahoo.com/group/capeverdeFORUM This is an active discussion group for topics related to Cape Verde and to the world wide Cape Verdean community

▶ www.expatscapeverde.com A useful resource that provides a service to both expats living and working in Cape Verde and to the islands

▶ www.capeverdetips.co.uk A site that provides some very useful travel information about visas, flights, travel between the islands hotels and medical facilities. It also has an extensive photo gallery and much more

VIDEOS

▶ www.youtube.com/carmensouza-videos Lisbon born Cape Verdean singer Carmen Souz regularly enchants her audiences no matter whether they are fans of jazz, chansons or world music. Sit back and enjoy her captivating voice singing the legendary 'Saudade'

Regardless of whether you are still preparing your trip or already on Cape Verde: these addresses will provide you with more information, videos and networks to make your holiday even more enjoyable

VIDEOS

▶ http://vimeo.com/20237166 This three minute video makes everything that is possible on the waves off the shores of Cape Verde immediately evident – no matter whether you are a board, wind or kite surfer

▶ short.travel/kav7 In this festival performance the young songwriter Techeka shows that male Cape Verdean musicians also have plenty to offer

APPS

▶ Over the Islands of Africa: Cape Verde – This iPhone, iPod touch, and iPad app features atmospheric photos taken by Stéphane Ducandas that capture the landscapes of the archipelago by land and by air

▶ Cape Verde Tour Book This tour guide offers a short introduction and brief, pithy information on Cape Verde's sights, history and culture, as well as prices and language, for all those who don't have any time for long internet searches

▶ Cape Verde Video The first android app about Cape Verde provides hundreds of videos along with some typical music

NETWORK

▶ http://streema.com/radios/country/Cape_Verde Put yourself in the mood by listening online to local radio stations

▶ www.airbnb.com Airbnb is the popular site for travellers who prefer to stay in private accommodation offered by locals. A search under Cape Verde pulls up the full spectrum from a waterfront apartment with views of the Atlantic in Mindelo through to a beautifully restored colonial house situated in the old part of Sal Rei on Boavista

▶ https://pt-br.facebook.com/CaboVerdeCV Those who speak Portuguese can communicate with other Cape Verde fans here and stay up to date; includes videos and photos

TRAVEL TIPS

ADDRESSES

Not all of the streets have names – not even in the larger towns – and those that do often don't have numbers. Addresses often only consist of the district and a nearby reference point.

ARRIVAL

To date, there are four international airports on the Cape Verdes: on the islands of Sal (SID), Boavista (BVC), Santiago (RAI) and São Vicente (VXE). From the UK there are direct flights to Sal and Boavista with Astraeus Airlines *(www.flyastraeus.com)* and Thompson *(flights.thomson.co.uk)* while from the United States there are weekly flights from Boston (BOS) to Praia (RAI) with Capo Verde Airlines (TACV, *www.flytacv.com*). The popular route is via Lisbon where there are regular direct flights with the Portuguese national airline TAP *(www.flytap.com)* and with TACV to Cape Verde. There are regular internal flights between Praia, Mindelo and Sal.

Should you travel by yacht then before you visit any of the other islands you are first required to clear into the country at one of the main ports – Palmeira (Sal), Praia (Santiago) or Mindelo (Sao Vicente). Failure to do so is punishable by a fine of up to 100,000 CVE (approx. £765/$1200).

BANKS & CURRENCY EXCHANGE

The currency is the Cape Verdean escudo (CVE). Its exchange rate is fixed to the euro (1 euro = 110.265 CVE) and may neither be brought into nor taken out of the country. Prices in simple restaurants and guesthouses are quite reasonable; everyday essentials are more expensive as everything has to be imported.
It will be easiest to carry the cash you need for the first days – exchange money at banks and Western Union branches – and then use your Visa card to withdraw cash. You should exchange some money before you leave the airport. Only large hotels accept credit cards.
There are banks in all of the larger towns; they have cash dispensers but most only accept Visa cards. You can also use these to get money at the bank counter *(Mon–Fri 8am–3pm)*.

CAR HIRE

Cars can be hired on almost all the islands. However, the roads, environment and driving habits might take some getting used to and the time and costs involved (high deposit) are significant. It is possible to

RESPONSIBLE TRAVEL

It doesn't take a lot to be environmentally friendly whilst travelling. Don't just think about your carbon footprint whilst flying to and from your holiday destination but also about how you can protect nature and culture abroad. As a tourist it is especially important to respect nature, look out for local products, cycle instead of driving, save water and much more. If you would like to find out more about eco-tourism please visit: *www.ecotourism.org*

hire a taxi or *aluguer,* with a local driver who knows his way around, for the same price as a hired car.

CONSULATES & EMBASSIES

There is no British Embassy in Cape Verde. If you need urgent assistance you should contact one of the British Honorary Consuls in Cape Verde or the British Embassy in Dakar, Senegal:

CAPE VERDE CONSULS
– Isabel Spencer, Honorary Consul for all islands except Sal and Boavista | tel. +238 232 35 12 or +238 232 31 23
– Albertino Mosso, Honorary Consul for Sal and Boavista | Santa Maria on Sal | tel. +238 995 10 or +238 595 73 83

BRITISH EMBASSY DAKAR, SENEGAL
BP 6025 Dakar | tel. +221 338 23 73 92 or 338 23 99 71 | www.gov.uk/government/world/organisations/british-embassy-dakar

EMBASSY OF THE UNITED STATES
Rua Abilio Macedo 6 | Caixa Postal 201 | Praia, Cape Verde | tel. +238 260 89 00 | praia.usembassy.gov

CUSTOMS

There are no restrictions on the import and export of foreign currency but it is forbidden to import or export Cape Verdean escudos. Duty free allowance includes the import of 200 cigarettes, 1L of spirits and 2L wine as well as items intended for your personal use, such as perfume.
The following goods can be exported duty-free when you leave Cape Verde: 200 cigarettes or 50 cigars or 250g tobacco,

BUDGETING

Water	£0.80/$1.30	*for a 1.5 litre bottle from a mini mercado*
Coffee	£0.80/$1.30	*for an espresso*
Guide	£24.50/$40	*for a tour of the Pico do Fogo*
Snack	£2/$3.30	*for a sandwich*
Music CD	£14.50/$23.50	*in a specialist shop*
Surfboard	£6.50/$10.50	*hourly hire rate*

1L of spirits or 4L wine, 250g coffee and other goods up to a value of £340/€430. Travellers to the US who are residents of the country do not have to pay duty on articles purchased overseas up to the value of $800, but there are limits on the amount of alcoholic beverages and tobacco products. For the regulations for international travel for US residents please see *www.cbp.gov*

DRINKING WATER

Tap water is not suitable for drinking and you should also use bottled water to brush your teeth. Check that the bottled water you are served in restaurants is still sealed.

ELECTRICITY

Electricity is not available everywhere and all the time. The decrepit network and old

CURRENCY CONVERTER

£	CVE	CVE	£
1	129	10	0.08
3	388	30	0.23
5	645	50	0.39
13	1.680	125	1
40	5.165	400	3.10
75	9.690	1,200	9.30
120	15.500	2,500	19.35
250	32.300	8,000	62
500	64.600	15,000	116

$	CVE	CVE	$
1	85	10	0.13
3	254	30	0.39
5	423	50	0.64
13	1,100	125	1.60
40	3,400	400	5.15
75	6,375	1,200	15.40
120	10,200	2,500	32
250	21,250	8,000	103
500	42,500	15,000	193

For current exchange rates see www.xe.com

technology means that there are often power failures lasting for hours or even days. Power is turned off in the small villages at 11pm or midnight. The voltage is 220 volt AC 50 Hz. The standard plugs are two pin.

EMERGENCY SERVICES

The free emergency numbers apply on all islands: hospital *tel. 130,* fire brigade *tel. 131,* police *tel. 132.*

HEALTH

There are chemists and clinics *(centro de saúde)* where a nurse or aid is available 24 hours a day on all the islands and there are state hospitals on Santiago, São Vicente, Santo Antão, Fogo and Sal. There is a considerable amount of bureaucracy and long waiting times. Private clinics are a convenient alternative for holidaymakers, and communication is often also easier. Chemists can be identified by a green cross sign and they usually have the most common used medicines. In spite of this, you should have a first-aid kit with you: good sunscreen, mosquito repellent, pain relievers and stomach settling medication are always a good idea.

National health schemes will usually not meet costs for treatment so it is advisable to take out private health insurance.

For more informations contact the National Travel Health Network and Centre *(www. nathnac.org/ds/c_pages/country_page_ CV.htm)* or the U.S. Department of State *(travel.state.gov/travel/cis_pa_tw/cis/ cis_1083.html).*

IMMIGRATION

All visitors require an entry visa. The application form can be downloaded from your respective Cape Verde Embassy website. In recent years, it has been possible to obtain the visa upon arrival at one of the country's four international airports. The current fee for such a visa is 2500 CVE but is subject to change. Your passport must be valid for at least another 6 months after your travel date.

CAPE VERDE CONSULATE UK
7A The Grove | London N6 6JU | tel. +44 78 76 23 23 05 | capeverde@jonathanlux.co.uk

**CAPE VERDE BUREAU –
UK AND IRISH REPUBLIC**
Suite 133, Imperial Court, Exchange Street | Liverpool L2 3AB | tel. +44 (0) 15 17 09 36 31 | www.capeverdebureau.com/cms

CAPE VERDE EMBASSY – USA
3415 Massachusetts Avenue | Washington DC 2007| tel. +1 (202) 965 68 20 | email: ambacvus@sysnet.net

INTERNET & WI-FI

Information about Cape Verde, photos and other links are available at the following internet addresses *www.capeverde. com, www.capeverdeweb.com*
Internet connections and cafés exist on all the islands but Wi-Fi is only available in the cities. However, the internet connection is often interrupted – sometimes for several days.

INTERNAL TRANSPORT

DOMESTIC FLIGHTS

With the exception of Santo Antão and Brava, all of the islands are serviced by TACV *(www.flytacv.com)*. It is essential that you confirm all your flights two days before departure in a TACV office or travel agency. The second national airline Halcyonair *(www.halcyonair.com)* flies to Sal, São Vicente, Santiago, Boavista and Fogo.

FERRIES

Ferries are especially suited for visiting the islands that have no airport, such as Brava and Santo Antão. The ferry to Santo Antão is reliable and departs twice daily; there is a ferry connection to Brava several times a week. The crossing takes about one hour. You will find Information on *www. capeverde.com/travel-tips/ferries.html*. A link for travellers with schedules between island ports can be found on *www.ferry lines.com/en/ferries/cape-verde*.

MEDIA

Listening to the radio is a widespread pastime – about 80 per cent of the resi-

Local women can carry incredible loads on their heads

dents do it every day. Broadcasts are in Portuguese and at some regional stations they are in Creole.
The two national newspapers 'A Semana' and 'Expresso das Ilhas' are published weekly in Portuguese. International press publications are only available at the international airports, if at all.

NOISE

Don't forget to pack earplugs in your luggage. The noise from the street, especially in city centres, can be very annoying late at night and early in the morning. There is usually also construction noise on Boavista and Sal. Dogs barking all night long is the rule, not the exception.

OPENING HOURS

Shops are open from 8am–1.30pm and from 3–6.30pm Monday to Friday and from 8am–1pm on Saturday, plus/minus half an hour; they are closed on Sunday and public holidays

PERSONAL SAFETY

Cape Verde is a safe country for travellers; however, there have been assaults on the beaches and secluded paths on those islands that are better developed for tourism. Do not make a show of expensive objects such as cameras, laptops and jewellery. It is safer to travel by taxi in Praia and Mindelo after dark.

PHONE & MOBILE PHONE

Post offices, hotels and many shops sell phone cards which you can use to make calls from one of the many payphones. Telephoning via the internet is the most economical method and is available in a cyber or telephone shop on most of the islands. Dialling codes are *+44* for the UK and *+1* for the USA; Cape Verde's dialling code is *+238* followed by the seven digit telephone number. Mobile phone reception functions for most European networks but the exorbitant charges make it only recommendable to be used in cases of emergency and for sending text messages. Telephoning home from the Cape Verdean network is also a pricy affair.

POST

There is a post and telephone station CTT in all major towns where you can purchase

WEATHER ON SAL

	Jan	Feb	March	April	May	June	July	Aug	Sept	Oct	Nov	Dec
Daytime temperatures in °C/°F	24/75	23/73	23/73	25/75	26/79	27/81	28/82	29/84	30/86	28/82	27/81	25/75
Nighttime temperatures in °C/°F	19/66	19/66	20/68	20/68	20/68	22/72	23/73	24/75	25/75	23/73	22/72	21/70
Sunshine hours/day	8	9	10	10	10	8	7	6	8	8	9	8
Precipitation days/month	1	1	1	0	0	2	3	3	4	3	1	1
Water temperatures in °C/°F	22/72	23/73	24/75	24/75	25/77	26/79	27/81	27/81	27/81	27/81	25/75	23/73

stamps, phone cards, make telephone calls (expensive) and post your letters. Opening hours *(as a rule, Mon–Fri 9am–1pm and 3–5pm)* can vary.

PUBLIC TRANSPORT

Aluguers travel between the larger towns and also connect villages with the next major communities. Ask where these shared taxis start from or flag one down on the road. Short trips cost around 100 CVE; the drivers have an official price list. There are also regular bus services in the town centre and suburbs of Mindelo and Praia.

SWIMMING

The rough surf and strong currents make swimming dangerous at many beaches. Only swim at designated beaches and pay attention to the flags: green = safe to swim, yellow = restricted swimming permitted, red = swimming prohibited.

TAXIS

The trip from the airports in São Vicente, Praia and Sal to the city centre or capital costs around 1000 CVE during the day. A small surcharge is added at night. There are fixed rates in the cities; e.g. a trip in the city area of Mindelo costs 200 CVE during the day; in the centre of Praia 200–400 CVE. A surcharge is also added at night.

TIME

Cape Verde is one hour behind Greenwich Mean Time (GMT), two hours during daylight saving time in summer; four hours ahead of US Eastern Time (EST) and seven hours ahead of Pacific Standard Time (PST), one hour plus during summer daylight saving time.

TIPPING

A tip of five to ten per cent is appropriate in restaurants if you were satisfied with the service. The porters at the ports and airports are available to help you for a small amount.

TOUR OPERATORS

Organising a trip to Cape Verde yourself will take a heavy toll on your time and nerves. In addition to local agencies, several operators are Cape Verde specialists.

CAPE VERDE TRAVEL

The UK agents for Capo Verde Airlines (TACV) offer a bespoke service to travellers to the islands. *Email sales@capeverde travel.com | www.capeverdetravel.*

THE CAPE VERDE SPECIALISTS

A well established tour operator whose team has first-hand knowledge of the islands. *www.capeverde.co.uk*

WEATHER, WHEN TO GO

Its pleasant tropical climate makes Cape Verde an ideal year-round holiday destination. Temperatures average between 21–29°C/70–84°F, plenty of sunshine from Nov–May and the rainy season is from June–Oct.

WHERE TO STAY

There are still no luxury hotels on all the islands, but there are guesthouses *(pensão/residêncial)* and private rooms. The standards vary greatly; some private accommodations are a match for those in a large hotel. The major hotels on the eastern islands that are well-developed for tourism.

USEFUL PHRASES KRIOLU

PRONUNCIATION

Most letters are pronounced the same as they are in English. The m at the end of a word is nasal, as are vowels marked with a circumflex (^). The following letter combinations correspond to the following sounds:

dj – j as in jungle, e.g. djuda (help)
j – s as in pleasure, e.g. paráji (stop)
nh – n as in onion, e.g. sánha (upset)
tx – ch as in chief, e.g. txábi (key)

Stress is on the penultimate syllable. Exceptions are words where the stressed syllable is marked by a tilde (~) or accent (´, ^), e.g. kafé (coffee) or kárga (luggage), as well as words ending in a consonant other than s (m, r, t etc.). These have the stress on the final syllable.

IN BRIEF

Yes/No/Maybe	Sin/Nau/Talves
Please/Thank you	Favor/Obrigádu
Excuse me, please	Diskulpâ-m
May I ...?/Pardon?	Posso?/Módi?
I would like to .../Have you got ...?	M-kré .../Tem ...?
How much is ...?	... é kántu?
I (don't) like that	M-(ka) gosta
good/bad	bon/mau
broken/doesn't work	stragádu
Help!/Attention!	Sakor!/Kutádu!
police/fire brigade	pulisia/bumbéru
Prohibition/forbidden	pruibidu
Danger/dangerous	pirigusu
Can I take your picture)/	Ta da pa-m tra-u fótu?
Can I take a picture?	Ta da pa-m fótu li?

GREETINGS, FAREWELL

Good morning!/afternoon!/	Bon diâ!/Boa tárdi!/
evening!/night!	Bo noti!
Hello!/Goodbye!	Olâ! Txau!
See you!	Txau!
My name is ...	M-txoma ...

Bu ta papia Kriolu?

"Do you speak Kriolu?" This guide will help you to say the basic words and phrases in Kriolu

What's your name?	Módi bu txoma?
I'm from ...	Mi é di ...

DATE & TIME

Monday/Tuesday/Wednesday	Sugunda-fera/Térsa-fera/Kuárta-fera
Thursday/Friday/Saturday	Kinta-fera/Sésta-fera/Sábru
Sunday/holiday	Diâ Dimingu/Feriadu
today/tomorrow/yesterday	oxi/manham/ónti
hour/minute	óra/minotu
day/night/week	diâ/noti/sumána

TRAVEL

open/closed	abertu/fexadu
entrance/exit	entrada/saida
departure/arrival	saida/txiga
toilets/restrooms /	kása-bánhu /
ladies/gentlemen	mudjer/ómi
(no) drinking water	(ka) águ bebi
Where is ...?/Where are ...?	Undi sta ...?
left/right/straight ahead	skérda/ndreta/frenti
near/far	pértu/lonji
bus / taxi/cab	otokáru / tákis
stop	paráji
parking lot	stasionamentu
street map/map	mápa
harbour/airport	portu/oroportu
ticket	bilieti
single/return	só di bai/bai ku bem
I would like to rent ...	M-kré luga ...
a car/a bicycle/a boat	káru/bisikléta/bárku
petrol/gas station	postu-gazulina
petrol/gas / diesel	gazulina / gazol
breakdown/repair shop	bariâ/ofisina

FOOD & DRINK

Could you please book a table for	Riserva um mesa pa kuátu alguém
tonight for four?	pa oxi, favor
on the terrace	na varanda
Could I please have ...?	M-ta toma ...

bottle/carafe/glass	garáfa/járu/kópu
salt/pepper/sugar	sal/margéta/sukri
with/without ice/sparkling	ku/sem gélu/okisijenádu
vegetarian/allergy	ka kumi kárni/alerjiâ
May I have the bill, please?	Tarsê-m kónta, favor
bill/receipt	kónta/risibu

SHOPPING

Where can I find ...?	Undi sta ...?
I'd like .../I'm looking for ...	M-kré .../M-sata djobi ...
Do you put photos onto CD?	Graba fótu na CD?
pharmacy	formása
baker/market	padariâ/merkádu
grocery/supermarket	lója/supermerkádu
photographic items/	lója du fótu/
newspaper shop/kiosk	papelariâ
100 grammes/1 kilo	100 grama/1 kilo
expensive/cheap/price	káru/barátu/présu
more/less	más/más poku

ACCOMMODATION

I have booked a room	A mi téni um kuártu riservadu
Do you have any ... left	Tem ...
single room/	um kuártu pa um algem
double room	um kuártu pa dós algem
breakfast/half board/	kafé/mei penson/
full board (American plan)	penson kumpletu
at the front/seafront	pa frénti/pa mar
shower/sit-down bath/terrace	xuveru/kása-bánhu/varanda
Is the power on?	Tem lus?

BANKS, MONEY & CREDIT CARDS

bank	bánku
pin code	sénha
I'd like to change ...	M-kré trokâ ...
cash/credit card	em notas/kartom vinti-kuátu
bill/coin	nóta/muéda

HEALTH

doctor/dentist/paediatrician	médiku/dentista/médiku mininu
hospital/emergency clinic	spital/postu-sakor
fever/pain	fébri/dor

USEFUL PHRASES

diarrhoea/nausea/sunburn	diariâ/bariga-báxu/kemadura sol
inflamed/injured	intxadu/firida
plaster/bandage	pénsu/algudom
cream/tablet/suppository	pomáda/kumprimidu/supozitóri

POST, TELECOMMUNICATIONS & MEDIA

stamp/letter/postcard	sélu/kárta/pustal
I need a landline phone card	A mi mésti um karton di tilifoni di tilifoni fixo
I'm looking for a prepaid card for my mobile	A mi sta ta prokura um karton di rikarga pam poi na telemóvi
Where can I find internet access?	La pundi um podi usa interneti?
Do I need a special area code?	A mi mésti um indikatif spezial?
dial/connection/engaged	diská/ligazon/interrumpid
socket/adapter/charger	tumada/adaptador/karregador
computer/battery/ rechargeable battery	komputador/pilha/ pilha rikarégavel
internet address (URL)/e-mail address	nderésu di interneti/nderésu di mail
internet connection/ wifi	adiri pa podi usa interneti/ interneti sem fio
e-mail/file/print	e-mail/fixeru/imprimi

LEISURE, SPORTS & BEACH

beach	rol-di-mar
sunshade/lounger	txapéu di sol/kadera pa diskanza
low tide/high tide/current	maré baxo/maré alto/kurenti

NUMBERS

0	zéru	15	kinzi
1	um	16	dizaséx
2	dós	17	dizaséti
3	trés	18	dizoitu
4	kuátu	19	dizanóvi
5	sinku	20	vinti
6	séx	21	vinti-um
7	séti	50	sunkuénta
8	oitu	100	sem
9	nóvi	200	duzéntus
10	dés	1000	mil
11	ónzi	2000	dós mil
12	duzi	10000	dés mil
13	treizi	½	um mei, metádi
14	katorzi	¼	um kuátu

NOTES

FOR YOUR NEXT HOLIDAY ...

MARCO POLO TRAVEL GUIDES

- PACKED WITH INSIDER TIPS
- BEST WALKS AND TOURS
- FULL-COLOUR PULL-OUT MAP
  AND STREET ATLAS

ROAD ATLAS

The green line ▬▬ indicates the Trips & Tours (p. 100–105)
The blue line ▬▬ indicates The perfect route (p. 30–31)

All tours are also marked on the pull-out map

Photo: Mountain range on Antão

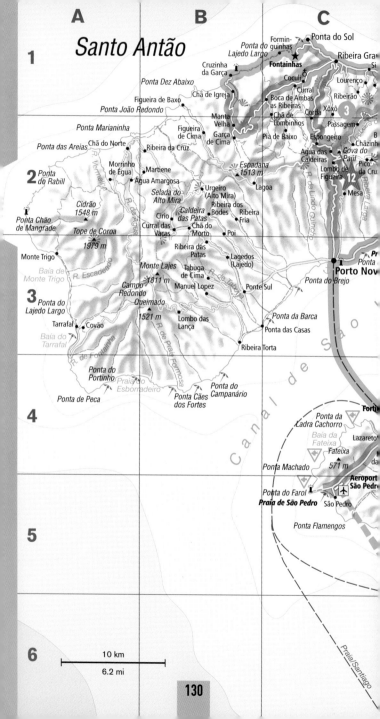

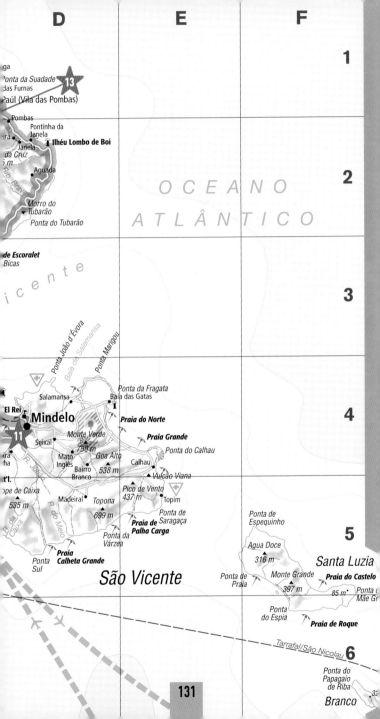

D **E** **F**

1

ga
Ponta da Suadade **13**
das Furnas
Paúl (Vila das Pombas)

Pombas
Pontinha da
Janela
ira ● ●Janela ⛰ **Ilhéu Lombo de Boi**
da Cruz
5 m
Aguada

O C E A N O

2

Morro do
▼ Tubarão
Ponta do Tubarão

A T L Â N T I C O

de Escoralet
Bicas

i c e n t e

3

Ponta João d'Évora
Baía de Salamansa
Ponta Marigou

Ponta da Fragata
Salamansa Baía das Gatas
El Rei ⚓
● **Mindelo** **i**
11 *Praia do Norte*

Monte Verde *Praia Grande*
Seixal *750 m* Ponta do Calhau
Mato Goa Alto
Inglês ▲ Calhau
Bairro *538 m*
Branco ▲ Vulcão Viana
Pico de Vento
pe de Caixa Madeiral ● Topona *437 m* Topim
535 m ▲ ●
699 m Ponta de
Praia de Saragaça
Praia da **Palha Carga**
Várzea

4

Ponta de
Espequinho

Ponta de
Espequinho

Agua Doce
Praia ▲
Ponta **Calheta Grande** *316 m*
Sul **Santa Luzia**

São Vicente Ponta de Monte Grande *Praia do Castelo*
Praia ▲ 85 m ● Ponta (
397 m Mãe Gr

Ponta
do Espia *Praia de Roque*

5

Tarrafal/São Nicolau

131

6

Ponta do
Papagaio
de Riba

Branco

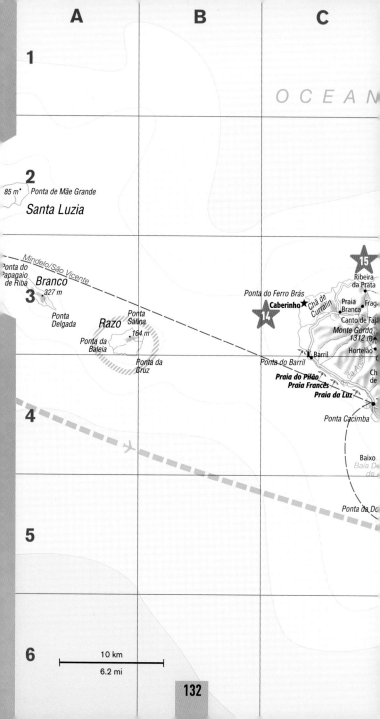

	A	B	C

1

OCEAN

2

85 m•   Ponta de Mãe Grande

Santa Luzia

Mindelo/São Vicente

Ponta do
Papagaio
de Riba   *Branco*
  327 m

3

Ponta
Delgada   *Razo*   Ponta
Salina
   164 m

Ponta da
Baleia

Ponta da
Cruz

Ponta do Ferro Brás

Ribeira
da Prata   **15**

Praia
Branca   Frag

Canto de Faja

Caberinho★ Chã de
Curralin

Monte Gordo
1312 m

Hortelão

14

Ponta do Barril   Barril   Ch
de

Praia do Pilão
Praia Francês
Praia da Luz

4

Ponta Cacimba

Baixo
Baia D
de

Ponta da Do

5

6   10 km
   6.2 mi

D **E** **F**

1

O ATLÂNTICO

2

São Nicolau

3

Ribeira Funda
Estância Bras
ada Fajã de
Baixo Carvoeiros
Queimadas
Fajã de
Cima
Cachaço Ribeira Brava
Lombinho Monte Bissau
615 m
eçalinho Calejão
iço Cachacinho
xo
Fontainhas
afal

Ponta
Coruja

Chã de Norte Belém Morro Brás
Alto Joaquinha
615 m

Ponta do
Juncalinho
Juncalinho

Ponta de
Plancão

Caldeira Morro Alto
Jalunga Castilhiano

Campo de
Preguiça
Ponta Galhana
Preguiça

Porto da Lapa
Baía da
Praia do Pito

Ponta
de Tope

Pico do Alberto
598 m

Centro de
Terra Chã

Ponta Pataca

Ponta Albacora

Praia Carriçal Baía
Gombeza

Carriçal

Ponta
Barroso

4

Chão Bonito
aixo 539 m Ponta Preta
cha

Baía da Fonte

Palmeira/Sal

adeira Ponta Grande

5

6

133

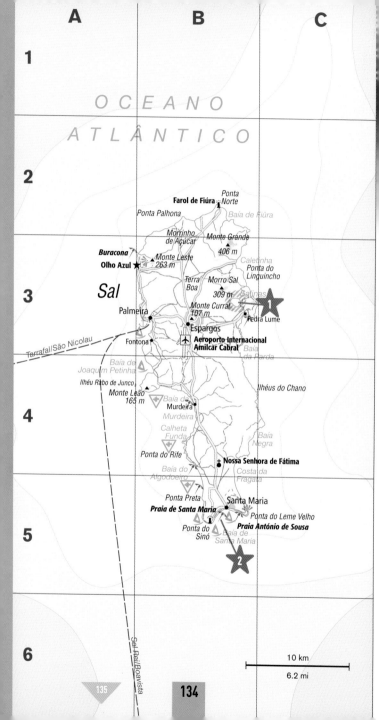

OCEANO
ATLÂNTICO

A B C

1

2

Ponta
Norte
Farol de Fiúra
Ponta Palhona *Baía de Fiúra*

Morrinho de Açúcar
Monte Grande
▲ *406 m*

Caletinha
Ponta do Linguincho

Buracona
Olho Azul ★
Monte Leste
263 m

Terra Boa
Morro Sal
▲ *309 m*
Salinas

Sal

Palmeira ●

Monte Curral
▲ *107 m*
★ 1
● Pedra Lume

Fontona ●
Espargos
✈ **Aeroporto Internacional Amilcar Cabral**

Baía da Parda

Tarrafal/São Nicolau
Baía de Joaquim Petinha

3

Ilhéu Rabo de Junco
Monte Leão
165 m
Baía de Murdeira
● Murdeira

Ilhéus do Chano

Calheta Funda

Baía Negra

4

Ponta do Rife
✝ **Nossa Senhora de Fátima** ●

Costa da Fragata

Baía do Algodoeiro

Ponta Preta
Praia de Santa Maria
ℹ
Ponta do Sinó
● Santa Maria
Ponta do Leme Velho
Praia António de Sousa
Baía de Santa Maria

★ 2

5

6

10 km
6.2 mi

135 ▽

134

Sal Rei/Boavista

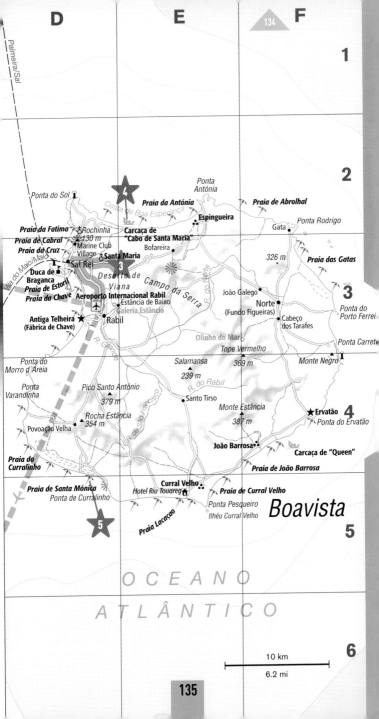

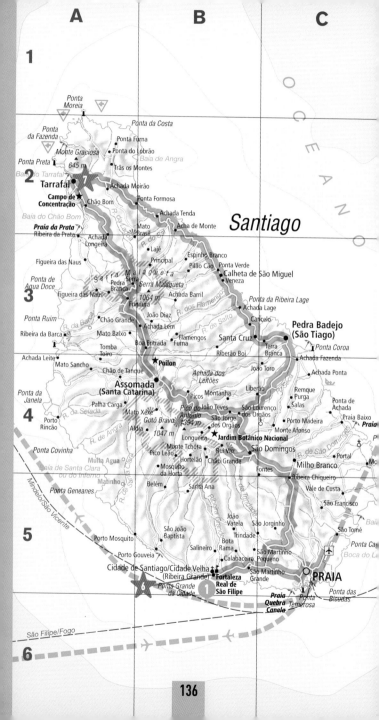

Santiago

	A	**B**	**C**

Ponta Moreia

Ponta da Costa

Ponta da Fazenda

Ponta Furna
Monte Graciosa
Ponta do Lobrão
Baía de Angra
645 m
Ponta Preta
Trâs os Montes

Baía do Tarrafal
Tarrafal
Achada Moirão
Campo de Concentração
Chão Bom
Ponta Formosa
Baía do Chão Bom
Achada Tenda
Praia da Prata
Acha de Monte
Ribeira da Prata
Mato Brasil
Achada Longeira
Lajé
Figueira das Naus
Principal
Espinho Branco
Ponta de Agua Doce
Serra
Pilão Cão
Ponta Verde
Serra Malagueta
Calheta de São Miguel
Pedra Branca
Veneza
Figueira das Naus
1064 m
Achada Barril
Ponta Ruim
Fundura
Ponta da Ribeira Lage
Chão Grande
João Diaz
Achada Lage
Ribeira da Barca
Achada Lém
Cancelo
Mato Baixo
Boa Entrada
Flamengos
Santa Cruz
Pedra Badejo (São Tiago)
Achada Leite
Tomba Toiro
Furna
Ribeirão Boi
Terra Branca
Ponta Coroa
Mato Sancho
Chão de Tanque
Poilon
Achada Fazenda
Ponta da Janela
Assomada (Santa Catarina)
Achada dos Leitões
João Toro
Achada Ponta
Picos
Montanha
Liberão
Remque
Purga
Salas
Palha Carga
Pico do João Teves
São Lourenço dos Orgãos
Ponta de Achada
Porto Rincão
Mato Xêxe
António
1394 m
São Jorge dos Orgãos
Porto Madeira
Praia Baixo
Gotô Bravo
1047 m
Monte Afonso
Praia
Ponta Covinha
Aldia
Jardim Botânico Nacional
Baía de Santa Clara ou do Inferno
Monte Tchôta
Rui Vaz
São Domingos
Milho Branco
Pico Leão
Hortelão
Chão Grande
Portal
Ponta Geneanes
Mosquito da Horta
Fontes
Ribeira Chiqueiro
Matinho
Belém
Santa Ana
Vale de Custa
João Varela
São Jorginho
São Francisco
São João Baptista
Trindade
Porto Mosquito
Salineiro
Bota Rama
São Tomé
Ponta Ca
Boca do L
Porto Gouveia
Calabaceira
São Martinho Pequeno
Cidade de Santiago/Cidade Velha (Ribeira Grande)
São Martinho Grande
PRAIA
Fortaleza Real de São Filipe
Ponta Grande da Cidade
Praia Quebra Canela
Ponta Temerosa
Ponta das Bicudas

Mindelo/São Vicente

São Filipe/Fogo

Santiago

OCEANO

Baía de Angra

R. de São Domingos

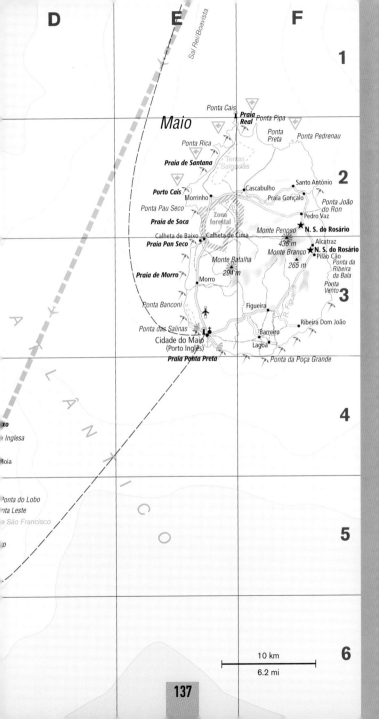

D

E

F

Sal Rei/Boavista

1

Maio

Ponta Cais

Praia Real

Ponta Pipa

Ponta Preta

Ponta Pedrenau

Ponta Rica

Terras Salgadás

Praia de Santana

Porto Cais

Morrinho

Cascabulho

Praia Gonçalo

Santo António

2

Ponta João do Ron

Pedro Vaz

Ponta Pau Seco

Zona forestal

Praia de Soca

Monte Penoso

N. S. do Rosário

Calheta de Baixo

Calheta de Cima

436 m

Alcatraz

N. S. do Rosário

Praia Pan Seco

Monte Branco

Pilão Cão

265 m

Ponta da Ribeira da Bala

Praia de Morro

Monte Batalha 294 m

Morro

Ponta Vento

3

Ponta Banconi

Figueira

R. Figueira

Ponta das Salinas

Ribeira Dom João

Cidade do Maio (Porto Inglês)

Barreiro

Lagoa

Praia Ponta Preta

Ponta da Poça Grande

xo

Inglesa

loia

4

Ponta do Lobo

nta Leste

e São Francisco

o

A T L Â N T I C O

5

10 km

6.2 mi

6

	A	B	C

1

O C E A N O

A T L Â N T I C O

2

3

Ilhéu Grande   *Ilhéus de Cima*

Ilhéu Luiz Carneiro

Ilhéus Secos ou do Rombo

Pont.

4

Ponta da Vaca

Baía da Pedrinha

Vila Nova Sintra

Furna

Cova Rodela

Monte Pesqueiro

Santa Bárbara

★ **Vinagre**

Fajã de Água

Cova Joana   Mato Grande

Ponta Espradinha   *N. S. do Monte*   João d'Nole

Baía do Porteto   *Lima Doce*   *Fontainhas 976 m*

Campo Baixo

Palhal   *Tantum*   *Cachaço*   **Brava**

Cova de Mar

Ponta do Alto

Ponta Nhô Martinho

5

6

10 km

6.2 mi

| D | E | F |

1

2

Fajãzinha
Laranjo
Ponta do Baixio
de Campanas
Ribeira Ilhéu
Mosteiros
Feijoal
Ponta da Salina
Las Salinas
Atalaia
Pai Antonio
Fonsaco
Ponta do Guincho
Campanas
de Baixa
São Jorge
Monte Velha
1209 m
Baía do Corvo
Galinheiro
Corvo
Ponta da Garça
Boca Larga
Rib. Filipe
Chã das
Caldeiras
8
Achada
Grande
*Baía de
Duas Pernas*
Torto Djo
Monte Verde
Bangaeira
Relva
Ponta Fundão
Achada
Lomba
R. da Lomba
Portela
★ **Cooperativa
Vinicola**
Ponta do Pesqueiro
Curral
Grande
Italiano
2
Pico de Fogo
Queimadinha
Monte Tabor
Zambuleiro
2829 m
9
Praia Casa
Ponta Praia Ladrão
R. de Sanha
Mira Mira
*Chã das
Caldeiras*
*Pico
Pequeno*
Na Stra da Cruz
Santo
Antônio
São Lourenço
Tinteira
Cidreira
ale de Cavaleiros
Coxo
*Monte Cruz
1800 m*
2
Tongom
*Lagariça
955 m*
Estância
Roque
Brandão
R. Vicente Dias
Coxo
Cabeça Fundão
Mãe
Joana
Bombardeiro
10
São Filipe
Vicente Dias
Monte Grande
Cova Figueira
a da Fonte Bila
Forno
Ponta da Areia
Patim
Achada Furna
Luzia Nunes
Batente
Monte
Larga
Fonte
Aleixo
Figueiro
Pavão
Fajã
**Projeto
Gênebra**
Salto
Dacabalaio
Nossa Senhora do Soccoro
Monte Vermelho
Baía de Nossa Senhora
Alcatraz
Baía de Pomba
Baía de Alcatraz
Ponta Matancia
Ponta Belcher
*Baía do
Carvalho*
Ponta Rachã
Fogo
Praia/Santiago

5

6

KEY TO ROAD ATLAS

....	Main road with number Hauptstraße mit Nummer
....	Secondary road Nebenstraßen
———————	Road unpaved Straße ungeteert
– – – – –	Road under construction Straße in Bau
....	Carriage way Fahrweg
–·–·–·–	Path Pfad
🏞	National park, nature reserve Nationalpark, Naturreservat
▽	Marine reserve Meeresschutzgebiet
⚓	Anchorage, harbour Ankerplatz, Hafen
⛵	Windsurfing Windsurfing
🚢	Wreck Schiffswrack
	Trips & Tours Ausflüge und Touren

♟	Castle Burg
♁ ♀	Church; chapel Kirche; Kapelle
▯	Lighthouse Leuchtturm
★	Point of interest Sehenswürdigkeit
∴	Archeological site Archäologische Stätte
▲	Mountain top Berggipfel
※ ※	Panoramic view Aussichtspunkt
⬡ ∘	Saline lake; well Salzsee/Saline; Quelle
🏖	Beach Badestrand
✈	International airport Internationaler Flughafen
✈	Aerodrome Flugplatz
	The perfect route Perfekte Route

MARCO POLO Highlights

INDEX

This index lists all islands, places, beaches, mountains and sights featured in this guide. Numbers in bold indicate a main entry.

WRITE TO US

e-mail: info@marcopologuides.co.uk

Did you have a great holiday?
Is there something on your mind?
Whatever it is, let us know!
Whether you want to praise, alert us
to errors or give us a personal tip –
MARCO POLO would be pleased to
hear from you.
We do everything we can to provide the
very latest information for your trip.

Nevertheless, despite all of our authors'
thorough research, errors can creep in.
MARCO POLO does not accept any
liability for this. Please contact us by
e-mail or post.

MARCO POLO Travel Publishing Ltd
Pinewood, Chineham Business Park
Crockford Lane, Chineham
Basingstoke, Hampshire RG24 8AL
United Kingdom

PICTURE CREDITS
Cover photograph: Sal, Santa Maria (Laif: Standl)
DuMont Bildarchiv: Schwarzbach (26 left, 28/29, 113); FFCB Arquitectos (16 bottom); Das Fotoarchiv: Schmidt (112); © fotolia.com: idreamphoto (17 top); Huber: Ripani (88), Schmid (2 centre top, 2 centre bottom, 2 bottom, 3 top, 3 centre, 7, 9, 10/11, 15, 26 right, 32/33, 34/35, 36, 40, 54/55, 60, 76/77, 78, 92, 100/101, 114 top, 141), Spila (21); mauritius images: Alamy (18/19, 48, 71, 91, 94/95, 112/113), Flüeler (4); H. Mielke (front flap left, 2 top, 3 bottom, 5, 12/13, 20, 23, 29, 30 bottom, 39, 42, 44, 47, 50, 53, 56, 65, 66, 69, 83, 96, 97, 98, 103, 106/107, 110, 110/111, 111, 114 bottom, 119, 128/129); Mito (16 top); D. Renckhoff (6, 30 top, 81, 109, 115); A. Rieck (1 bottom, 72, 75); T. Stankiewicz (front flap right, 8, 24/25, 27, 58, 63, 84/85, 87, 104); TransCity: Michael Neville (16 centre); Villa Botanico (17 bottom)

1st Edition 2014
Worldwide Distribution: Marco Polo Travel Publishing Ltd, Pinewood, Chineham Business Park, Crockford Lane, Basingstoke, Hampshire RG24 8AL, United Kingdom. E-mail: sales@marcopolouk.com
© MAIRDUMONT GmbH & Co. KG, Ostfildern
Chief editor: Marion Zorn
Author: Annette Rieck; editor: Ulrike Frühwald
Programme supervision: Ann-Katrin Kutzner, Nikolai Michaelis
Picture editor: Gabriele Forst
What's hot: wunder media, Munich
Cartography road atlas & pull-out map: DuMont Reisekartografie, Fürstenfeldbruck; © MAIRDUMONT, Ostfildern
Design: milchhof : atelier, Berlin; Front cover, pull-out map cover, page 1: factor product munich
Translated from German by Robert McInnes; editor of the English edition: Margaret Howie, fullproof.co.za
Prepress: M. Feuerstein, Wigel
Phrase book: Annette Rieck

DOS & DON'TS ✋

Things to look out for in Cape Verde

DO EXPECT A RELAXED ATTITUDE TO TIME

Some things on Cape Verde are fundamentally different and one such example is the approach to time. An hour earlier or later, or a day more or less is not so important. You should leave any expectations you have about punctuality and reliability at home – and always have something to read with you to help you pass the time while you are waiting (at the airport, etc).

DON'T SHOW TOO MUCH SKIN

Being seen naked in public is considered indecent in Cape Verde. Save the passing fishermen and other people at the beach any embarrassment and only swim or sunbathe topless where it is tolerated: in the hotel district in Santa Maria.

DON'T ABUSE HOSPITALITY

It goes without saying that the guest is always given the best the house has to offer. Accept any present graciously but return the favour. You should never take advantage of any hospitality you are offered such as staying for a lengthy period without recompensing. And, try to give your gifts when nobody else is around.

DON'T TRESPASS ON NATURE

Many of the animals and plants on the Cape Verde Islands are now very rare and some are even threatened with extinction. Allow the few birds, reptiles, insects, herbs and plants their last refuges – the uninhabited islands and designated nature reserves. You should also not visit the turtle beaches on your own initiative. Take advantage of the offers provided by the environmental protection organisations – they provide information and organise visits – and you will learn far more that way.

DO AVOID BUYING TURTLE PRODUCTS

Never buy any souvenirs or other products derived from turtles. They always cost the life of one of the few existing animals. And, most governments also prohibit their import making them illegal for you to take home.

DON'T UNDERESTIMATE THE SUN

At these latitudes, the sun is so intense that it can be a real danger for pale skin. And the constant breeze eases the heat but increases the risk of sunburn. Always use a sunscreen with a high protection factor – even if it is cloudy. And always take a hat.